The Macat Library
世界思想宝库钥匙丛书

解析约翰·P.科特
《领导变革》

AN ANALYSIS OF
JOHN P. KOTTER'S
LEADING CHANGE

Yaamina Salman   Nick Broten ◎ 著

曾文雄 ◎ 译

上海外语教育出版社
外教社 SHANGHAI FOREIGN LANGUAGE EDUCATION PRESS

目　录

CONTENTS

引言

要 点

- 约翰·P. 科特生于 1947 年，是美国管理顾问 * 和学者，目前在哈佛商学院讲授领导力 * 与管理 * 课程，并通过他的公司科特国际向各类组织提供咨询服务。

- 《领导变革》展示了一个全面的八步骤模式，为大企业的组织变革提供解决方案。

- 该书采用真实案例，适用广泛，是最具影响力的组织转型图书之一。

约翰·P. 科特其人

约翰·P. 科特是组织变革与转型领域的标志性人物，蜚声学术界和商业界。他在该领域著述颇丰，并广为商业界和学术界人士传阅与肯定。他常被誉为企业变革与管理领域的权威。[1]科特在写作中大量采用其作为企业管理顾问的从业经历，其整个职业生涯的实践经验，包括他从领导力和管理咨询工作和对可行方案的研究中获得的经验，都成为他的著述基础。管理转型是科特几十年来的主要关注点之一。与科特的其他著作类似，《领导变革》一书巧用人物轶事和实例分析，以对话口吻娓娓道来，就好像直接与企业高管和商界领导交谈一般。

科特生于 1947 年，曾获麻省理工学院学士和硕士学位，1972年在哈佛大学商学院获博士学位。1980 年成为哈佛大学的专职教授，时年 33 岁，成为哈佛大学历史上最年轻的教授之一。后来，科特任哈佛商学院"松下幸之助"领导力荣休教授，讲授领导力与管理课程。此外，他还是科特国际咨询公司的董事长和联合创始人。该公司始创于 2008 年，拥有广泛的客户群，与好事达、基因泰克、微软等公司以及美国海军航空系统司令部、加拿大皇家海军等政府部门均有业务来往。[2]

《领导变革》的主要内容

《领导变革》于 1996 年第一次出版，涵盖两大核心部分。首先，科特分析了企业在试图变革时所犯的 8 种最常见错误：

1. 放任自满情绪，未能激发迫切感。

2. 未能组建行之有效的领导联盟（志同道合者的联盟）。

3. 未能构建合理的愿景。

4. 对变革的愿景沟通不足。

5. 容许阻碍愿景实现的因素存在，例如滞后的组织结构和顽抗的员工。

6. 未能以短期成效为基础来深化变革。

7. 过早宣告胜利。

8. 未能将成功的变革融入企业文化 *。

科特指出，"在一个节奏缓慢、竞争微弱的社会中，我们无需为上述错误付出高昂的代价。"[3] 但是，处在经济快速变化的时代，"犯这八种常见错误中的任何一种，其后果都非常严重。"[4] 变革过于缓慢会造成裁员和预算紧张等现象，并会持续影响企业所在的社区。

为了引导公司规避这些错误，科特详述了领导变革的八个步骤。这些步骤必须按以下顺序实施：

1. 树立紧迫感。

2. 组建领导联盟 *。

3. 设计愿景与战略。

4. 传达变革愿景。

5. 全面授权赋能 *。

6. 创造短期成效 *。

7. 巩固成果并深化变革。

8. 将新途径根植于企业文化中。[5]

对管理与领导力的区分是科特变革八步骤的另一显著特征。科特认为，"成功转型需要 70%—90% 的领导力加 10%—30% 的管理。"[6] 他指出，在节奏缓慢的社会里，管理人才可能比领导力更重要。"在 20 世纪的大部分年代里，我们在人类历史上首次创造出成千上万个大型组织，却没有培养出足够多的优秀管理者来掌管好这些官僚组织。"[7] 恰恰相反，在技术和工业转型的时代，成功转型要求变革者具备"舍身忘我、甘心奉献和富有创造力"[8] 的优良品质；与其说这是对管理者的要求，毋宁说是对领导者的要求。

《领导变革》的核心是科特精心设计的变革八步骤和相关实例分析。在构建领导联盟一节中谈及的"杰瑞"就是其中一个典型实例。杰瑞是一位"工作过度的大石油公司区域首席财务官（CFO）"[9]，但更像是一位"管理者而不是领导者"，所以他自然而然地对重大变革的呼吁充满了怀疑。因而初看之下，似乎不值得努力说服他支持变革。他很可能会抵抗，也可能不会提供任何创造性的解决办法。[10] 然而杰瑞在公司身居要职，拥有一定资历，工作经验丰富，如果将他排除在变革联盟之外，结果会适得其反。因此，科特建议领导者将"杰瑞"纳入变革规划中。"杰瑞式人物"在《领导变革》中随处可见。很大程度上，这本书的成功得益于这些穿插其中的人物以及对这些人物境况的细致剖析。

《领导变革》的学术价值

《领导变革》是不可多得的资源，适合各类读者群。对组织转型相关问题有所了解的商务专业学生可以直接借鉴书中的相关实例和概念。科特所列举的案例犹如真实的商务案例：目前所讨论的市场是什么样的？涉及什么样的人物？科特是如何分析这些人物所犯的错误的？对其进行考察与分析，学生可从中受益。有志于担任高层领导的商务专业学生能从中掌握变革方法，这些方法是由过去 20 年中最具影响力的变革咨询专家之一的科特所提出的。完全领会科特理念的学生在进入职场后，与自己的老板打交道应更得心应手。

这本书也是非商务专业学生的好帮手。《领导变革》中的大多数原则适用于任何组织环境。例如，科特指导变革的领导者如何沟通愿景："力求简明"，"重点明确，无行业术语"，且运用"隐喻、类比、事例或丰富多彩的语言，以迅速有效地传达复杂的思想。"[11]科特的理念适用于实施变革的大公司，也适用于初创公司、新的营销活动、国会竞选以及大学里的重大研究项目。可以说，来自各种团体的读者群，无论团体规模大小、职能如何，都能从《领导变革》中获得真知灼见。

科特本能地认为领导力比管理更重要。《领导变革》末章所论及的"终身学习者"*模式旨在应对个人和职业持续发展的挑战。科特使用了复合成长*（基于自身的不断发展）概念对个人发展作了讨论，他提出，诸如征求他人的评价反馈或勇于冒险等细节行为的变化能够促成个人的重大转变。[12]简言之，《领导变革》不仅可作为商业界的实用性参考书，也可被视为一本励志书籍。

1. "科特的八个变革步骤模式"，思维工具，登录日期 2015 年 5 月 21 日，https://www.mindtools.com/pages/article/newPPM_82.htm。

2. "我们的客户"，科特国际，登录日期 2015 年 5 月 17 日，https://www.kotterinternational.com/clients/。

3. 约翰·P.科特：《领导变革》，波士顿：哈佛商学院出版社，1996 年，第 15 页。

4. 科特：《领导变革》，第 15 页。

5. 科特：《领导变革》，第 20—22 页。

6. 科特：《领导变革》，第 26 页。

7. 科特：《领导变革》，第 27 页。

8. 科特：《领导变革》，第 30 页。

9. 科特：《领导变革》，第 60 页。

10. 科特：《领导变革》，第 60 页。

11. 科特：《领导变革》，第 91—92 页。

12. 科特：《领导变革》，第 183 页。

第一部分：学术渊源

1 作者生平与历史背景

要点 🔑

- 《领导变革》介绍了成功实施组织变革的八个步骤。

- 科特在许多不同行业担任管理顾问的经历，使这本书匠心独运，颇具实用价值。

- 这本书 1996 年首次出版，正值全球化*日益深化之时，人们对全球化将给商业运作带来什么变化众说纷纭。

为何要读这部著作？

约翰·P. 科特"领导变革：转型为何失败"[1] 一文发表在《哈佛商业评论》1995 年 3—4 月刊上，深受读者欢迎，且影响深远。次年，在此基础上，科特写就《领导变革》。这本书荣获颇多奖项，跃居国际畅销书，成为领导力和变革领域具有里程碑意义的著作。它立足于作者在大公司的咨询经验，致力于促进组织的成功转型，其核心理念是实施变革的八个步骤。"大"是书中一个重要的概念，《领导变革》聚焦于大公司而非小企业的转型问题。

风格平实，切近实际，是这本书的显著优势。科特抛开学究式论证，简明扼要地论述了变革原则，并常常引用名不见经传的真实公司的案例，以支持其观点。这本书用例广泛，指导性强，吸引了广泛的读者群。虽然并非所有读者都会认可变革的八个步骤，但有大公司工作经历的读者应会发现至少其中的一些建议非常有用。另外，《领导变革》以其前瞻性而著称。当前商业环境快速变化，全球化趋势方兴未艾，正是在这一背景之下，科特提出了关于组织变革的论述。他所关注的有关如何应对迅速变化的理念，即便在当下仍具很强的适用性。

> "在过去 20 多年里，无论使用何种客观指标来衡量，各类组织所进行的重大且往往引发震荡的变革次数显著增加。尽管有些人预测，大多数的流程再造、战略调整、兼并收购、精简裁员、质量提升、文化再造等工程将很快消失，但是，我认为这种可能性极低。……结果就是，这会促使越来越多的组织降低成本，提升产品质量，提高服务水平，寻求新的增长机会并提高生产率。"
>
> —— 约翰·P. 科特：《领导变革》

作者生平

约翰·P. 科特生于 1947 年，1968 年毕业于麻省理工学院电子工程和计算机科学专业，此后获得麻省理工学院理学硕士与哈佛商学院工商管理博士。1972 年，科特在哈佛商学院任教，1980 年晋升为全职教授，时年 33 岁。他至今仍在该学院任教。

纵观其职业生涯，科特已出版 18 部著作，其中包括 2006 年出版的《纽约时报》畅销书《冰山在融化》。基于对 504 家企业的调查数据，[2]《商业周刊》在 2001 年将科特评选为美国"领导力大师第一人"。科特也是科特国际咨询公司的创始人，该公司为"全球 5 000 家公司"*数据库提供咨询服务，帮助这些产出超过 50 万亿美元营收额的大企业按书中介绍的"领导变革的八个步骤"实施变革。

据科特所言，《领导变革》的写作素材全部源自其为近 100 家企业长达 25 年的商业咨询实战经验。正如他在这本书的前言中所述："与之前出版的书相比，本书更注重个人的亲身经历；我希望传达我的所见所闻以及对日益重要的一系列关联议题的思考和结论。"[3] 从公开描述的实例看，我们无从得知科特咨询工作的确切性质，也无法了解他与书中实例所涉公司之间的具体关系。但是，科特在领导力和变革管理领域享有国际盛誉，作为组织变革的思想先驱，他对真实案例的阐释自然能令人信服。

创作背景

快速的技术变革*、国际经济一体化*、发达国家的国内市场*发展变化——全球化浪潮深刻影响了科特的作品。20 世纪 80 年代兴起的现代全球化浪潮与诸多事件相联系，包括一系列自由贸易*协定。这些协定打破了全球贸易壁垒，减少了运输成本，促使企业转向海外发展，以降低生产成本。这些都形成了《领导变革》的创作背景。

科特指出，企业难以摆脱全球化经济力量和社会力量的影响，因此组织变革的愿望更为强烈。虽然在 20 世纪全球化兴起之前，企业几乎无需内部转型，都能生存数十年，但科特声称，在市场全球化的时代，此类情况将不复出现。他写道："即使是那些仅在小区域内营销的公司，也能感受到全球化带来的冲击。有时候这种冲击是间接的：丰田汽车公司打败了通用汽车公司，于是通用汽车公司裁员，通用员工只好省吃俭用，还要求街角的干洗店提供更加优惠的服务。"[4] 这个事例突显出，在全球化的市场中，商业决策可能会造成意想不到的后果。丰田汽车公司的决策以利己为取向，但其决策直接影响到通用汽车公司，而后间接影响许多小型企业，包括为通用员工提供服务的干洗店。

1. 约翰·P.科特："领导变革：转型为何失败",《哈佛商业评论》第73卷，1995年第2期，第59—67页。

2. "管理大师评级"，布隆伯格，2001年10月14日，登录日期2015年5月18日，https://www.bloomberg.com/bw/stories/2001-10-14/rating-the-management-gurus。

3. 约翰·P.科特：《领导变革》，波士顿：哈佛商学院出版社，1996年，第x页。

4. 科特：《领导变革》，第18页。

2 学术背景

要点 ⌐⊶╍

- 对管理的研究涉及规划、结构、设计以及机构的有效性，尤其是商业组织的有效性；《领导变革》关注变革项目，论及上述诸多议题。

- 科特出版这本书之前，管理学*的焦点已从研究管理目标转向研究管理层与员工的关系。

- 《领导变革》的创作素材源自科特本人的工作经历，但很可能受到同时期类似变革模式的影响。

著作语境

约翰·P.科特的《领导变革》是管理学的经典之作。管理学作为商业思想的一个领域，关注组织（尤其是公司）如何规划和分配资源，以实现预定的目标。一个与此相关（有时甚至重叠）的学科是领导力研究*，专注于组织目标执行中的领导力作用。管理学与领导力研究大致分为两大类：一类是对组织行为*的高度理论化（有时涉及数学运算）研究；另一类为面向商业领导的实用指南。《领导变革》就是第二类的典范之作。

《领导变革》也属于更宽泛的商业与管理类图书。这一类型的学术写作可兼备分析性与规定性，针对学界和商界读者。例如，作者可以开展广泛的调研项目，包括调查和统计分析，以判断激励机制对公司业绩产生的影响。此类研究分析包含通过观察得到的结果，与经济学*和政治学*的研究发现相似。在某些局面不确定的时期，有学者也许会结合真实世界的实例与自己的灵感写一部管理者指南。就其本质而言，商业文献丰富多样，研究方法交叉融合众多学科，诸如经济学、社会学、数学和历史学等学科。

> "管理者正确地做事，领导者做正确的事。"
> —— 彼得·德鲁克：《德鲁克管理思想精要：管理、个人与社会》

学科概览

现代管理学可追溯到彼得·德鲁克*的研究，德鲁克是奥地利裔美国管理咨询专家、学者。在 1954 年出版的《管理的实践》中，德鲁克提出的目标管理*方法是其对该领域最卓著的贡献。目标管理理论要求管理者作出决策，领导组织完成特定目标，同时要重视外部环境的变化，例如经济波动和市场上其他公司的行动。德鲁克认为，只有提前确定目标，决策才能行之有效。"任何一个领域都需要设定目标，绩效和结果对企业的生存和发展有着直接的、举足轻重的影响。"[1] 虽然管理者作决策时可能更喜欢尽量简化程序，且不希望他人评估，以此限制可供选择的范围来减少错误，但是德鲁克认为，运用评估手段是成功管理最重要的方面之一。

道格拉斯·麦格雷戈*是另一位致力于管理学与领导力早期研究的学者。在 1960 年出版的《企业的人性面》中，他提出了"X理论和 Y 理论"*个人动机模型。[2] 在此语境下，"理论"指的是管理者对员工所作的一种假设——换言之，管理者以先入为主的激励理论对待员工。根据麦格雷戈的观点，X 理论假设员工懒惰消极，逃避工作，因而需严密监督，而 Y 理论则假设员工积极向上，自我激励。麦格雷戈向管理者介绍，公司绩效受到管理层对员工个人动机假设的影响。此外，麦格雷戈还将心理学、行为学的概念引入了管理学研究。

学术渊源

20 世纪 90 年代，正值科特构思《领导变革》之际，市场上已有越来越多的类似著作论及所谓学习型组织 *（重视团队合作与协同管理模式）、组织变革和广义的转型等问题。例如，W. 沃纳·伯克 * 和乔治·利特文 * 创建了一个模型，试图描述成功变革项目的共同特征。[3] 与科特的著作不同，伯克和利特文探索变革的成因，而非管理者如何更好地实施变革。希瑟·哈夫曼 *1992 年发文反驳变革有损于组织绩效的观点。她指出，"如果是为了应对环境条件的重大重组，并且是建立在既定的程序和能力之上，那么组织变革有利于提升组织绩效，拓展可能的生存空间。"[4] 换言之，如果环境迫使公司实施变革，公司往往能从中获益；反之，变革则可能会造成伤害。

同时期，彼得·圣吉 * 和威廉·爱德华兹·戴明 * 等学者也在积极探索变革情景下的质量控制、团队合作与适应性组织。[5] 圣吉和戴明都意识到全球化的重要性以及全球化带来的挑战。诚然，面对复杂的全球经济，戴明给管理者的忠告之一是："取消目标管理"，而"以领导力代之"。[6] 科特无疑受到上述学者的影响。不过，在《领导变革》中，他并没有直接做出回应，而是将他们的一些思想融入该书。需要指出的是，科特的《领导变革》主要源自其自身的经历与灵感，而不是他人的著述。

1. 彼得·德鲁克:《管理的实践》,纽约:哈珀柯林斯出版社,1954 年,第 63 页。

2. 道格拉斯·麦格雷戈:《企业的人性面》,纽约:麦格劳-希尔出版社,1960 年。

3. W. 沃纳·伯克和乔治·H. 利特文:"组织绩效与变革因果关系模型",《管理学期刊》第 18 卷,1992 年第 3 期,第 523—545 页。

4. 希瑟·A. 哈夫曼:"岩石与硬地之间:基本环境变革条件下的组织变革与绩效",《管理科学季刊》第 37 卷,1992 年第 1 期,第 48 页。

5. 彼得·M. 圣吉:《第五项修炼:学习型组织的艺术与实践》,伦敦:世纪商业出版社,1991 年;威廉·爱德华兹·戴明:《转危为安》,马萨诸塞州坎布里奇:麻省理工学院出版社,2000 年。

6. 戴明:《转危为安》,第 24 页。

3 主导命题

要点 🔑

- 20 世纪 90 年代，学界关注组织变革的内容、情境和过程。

- 同时期提出的其他变革模式，虽与《领导变革》中的模式类似，但仅重视变革过程的各个不同方面。

- 科特敏锐地观察到同一领域的其他变革模式，但没有直接拿来就用。

核心问题

约翰·P.科特的《领导变革》于 20 世纪 90 年代出版之际，正值全球化兴起，商业环境变化迅猛，组织变革自然成为当时的热门话题。此时的学者主要围绕三大主题讨论组织变革：[1]

变革内容：力图描述导致变革成败的共同因素（可参考 W. 沃纳·伯克和乔治·利特文的模型以及托马斯·沃尔曼*的论述）。[2]

变革情境：考察组织内外部环境的各种动力和条件，分析它们是如何影响变革过程的（可参考尼尔斯·芬斯塔德*、希瑟·哈夫曼的论述）。[3]

变革过程：专注分析从外部环境、公司、个人层面引发变革的实际行动（可参看库尔特·勒温*、蒂莫西·加尔平*、阿喀琉斯·A.阿米纳基斯*等人的著述）。[4]重点在于改善变革过程，而非仅仅理解变革过程。

科特的《领导变革》一书涉及上述第三个议题，明确了在个人和公司层面所要执行的一系列行为，界定了组织变革实施过程的各个阶段。科特研究的核心问题是：哪些因素妨碍大型组织变革项目顺利实施？可采取哪些步骤来提高组织实施变革的能力？显然，把握此情境下"变革"的意蕴，尤为重要。在科特看来，"变革"意味着"机构重组、流程再造、战略调整、兼收并购、精简人员、质量监控、文化再造"。[5] 换言之，"变革"是指任何企业结构或功能的改良。科特并非唯一提出这一问题的学者，但其视野开阔、分析透彻，使其观点具有鲜明的独创性，从而更贴近学界和商界人士。

> "据说，抗拒全球化，就如同抗拒万有引力定律。"
> ——《全球主义者》："科菲·安南论全球的未来"

参与者

阿诺德·贾德森 * 和蒂莫西·加尔平两位学者于20世纪90年代出版的著作与科特的《领导变革》相类似。贾德森提出的模式包含实施变革的五个阶段：

1. 分析和计划变革。
2. 沟通传达变革。
3. 接纳新行为。
4. 实现从现状到理想状态的转变。
5. 巩固新成效。[6]

贾德森模式的一个关键要素是：提供奖励方案和激励措施，以尽量减少管理者的消极抵抗。这种理念是科特模式所欠缺的。

加尔平提出另一指引实施变革过程的模式。[7] 他的模式并非一系列关键阶段，而是犹如由九个楔子组成的轮子。这个楔子模式如下：

1.确立变革需求。

2.构建和分享变革愿景。

3.分析当前形势。

4.提出建议。

5.细化建议。

6.试点检验建议。

7.准备推出建议。

8.正式推出建议。

9.评估、强化和改进变革。

加尔平模式与科特模式类似。贾德森模式、加尔平模式和科特模式三者确有相似之处；尽管它们的终极目标都是将变革融入企业文化，但各模式的侧重点明显不同。

当代论战

虽然科特可能注意到同时期其他学者有关组织变革方面的著作，但《领导变革》及作为其基础的刊发在《哈佛商业评论》上的文章都没有直接引用该领域的其他著作。事实上，《领导变革》没有提供任何参考文献，科特的论述全部源自其个人经历和灵感。与学界前辈不同，科特全面地勾勒出一个完整的、自始至终的变革过程。

在没有引用其他学术著作的情况下，科特以《领导变革》为驰骋思想的平台，将《变革的力量：领导力与管理的差异》和《企业文化与业绩》等以往著作的观点都纳入其中。[8] 正如他在前言中写道："与我之前出版的作品不同，《领导变革》没有脚注和尾注；除了我自己的作品外，书中既没有引用任何其他出版物的实例或主要观点，也没有试图引用其他来源的事实例证来支持我的结论。"[9]这一做法使《领导变革》有别于同时期的其他同类图书。

1. 阿喀琉斯·A.阿米纳基斯、阿瑟·G.贝代安："组织变革：20世纪90年代的理论与研究综述"，《管理学杂志》第25卷，1999年，第293—315页。

2. 参见W.沃纳·伯克、乔治·H.利特文："组织绩效与变革因果关系模型"，《管理学杂志》第18卷，1992年第3期，第523—545页；托马斯·E.沃尔曼：《转型势在必行：通过激进变革实现市场支配》，波士顿：哈佛商学院出版社，1996年。

3. 尼尔斯·芬斯塔德："组织变革的修辞学"，《人际关系》第51卷，1998年第6期，第717—740页；希瑟·A.哈夫曼："岩石与硬地之间：基本环境变革条件下的组织变革与绩效"，《管理科学季刊》第37卷，1992年第1期，第48—75页。

4. 库尔特·勒温："群体动力学前沿Ⅱ：群体生活的渠道；社会规划与行动研究"，《人际关系》第1卷，1947年，第143—153页；蒂莫西·J.加尔平：《变革的人性面：组织重新设计的实用指南》，旧金山：乔西-巴斯出版社，1996年；阿喀琉斯·A.阿米纳基斯、斯坦利·G.哈里斯和休伯特·S.费尔德："组织变革范式：变革主体与变革目标视角"，《公共行政和公共政策》第87卷，2001年，第631—658页。

5. 约翰·P.科特：《领导变革》，波士顿：哈佛商学院出版社，1996年，第ix页。

6. 阿诺德·S.贾德森：《组织行为变革：将抵触变革的阻力最小化》，马萨诸塞州坎布里奇：布莱克威尔出版社，1991年。

7. 加尔平：《变革的人性面》。

8. 约翰·P.科特：《变革的力量：领导力与管理的差异》，纽约：自由出版社，1990年；约翰·P.科特、詹姆斯·L.赫斯克特：《企业文化与业绩》，纽约：自由出版社，1992年。

9. 科特：《领导变革》，第x页。

4 作者贡献

要点 ⚿

- 《领导变革》基于 1995 年刊登在《哈佛商业评论》的同名文章拓展而成，科特在该文中勾勒了实施组织变革的八个步骤。

- 科特遵循简洁平实的行文方式，先介绍变革步骤，接着用实例解析，并通过讨论来详述。

- 尽管克里斯·阿吉里斯*、道格拉斯·麦格雷戈等学者有关变革的著作探索了类似的领域，但《领导变革》主要立足于科特的前期著述。

作者目标

约翰·P.科特撰写《领导变革》一书旨在拓展 1995 年刊登在《哈佛商业评论》的文章"领导变革：转型为何失败"中的思想。[1]该文颇受读者欢迎，跃居《哈佛商业评论》重印榜首位。读者的反响促使科特继续探索变革这个主题："第一，管理者可以了解到组织在力图真正实现变革之际常犯的错误，然后说，这些错误正是变革成效远未达到预期目标的根源！第二，读者感受到领导变革八个步骤模式富有说服力、引人入胜。"[2]为了更好地扩展该文的思想，科特引用了"数十个实例，包括成功的和失败的案例"。[3]这些案例不但为全书增添了趣味，还清晰地呈现了科特思想背后的愿景，使其论述更令人信服。

纵观全书，科特按其构思自由驰骋，勾勒出切实可行的变革"路线图"。这本书的目标读者为高管群体，旨在为高管实施组织变革做准备——若无经验或指南可循的话，变革往往会令人望而生畏。由于科特描述的是自上而下展开的步骤，普通员工会觉得这些步骤与他们的实践经验不甚相关。的确，根据科特的变革模式，实施变革的主要责任人是组织的高管，而非企业的基层员工。事实上，《领导变革》持续畅销，说明它仍是管理者的核心读物，而且书中的事例既恰如其分又切合实际。

> "1994 年夏，我给《哈佛商业评论》写了篇名为'领导变革：转型为何失败'的文章，素材源自过去 15 年间我所分析的数十个推进组织重大变革的方案。……正值该文杀青之际，我希望就这个主题做更深入的探索，故不久后开始了本书的写作。"
>
> ——约翰·P. 科特：《领导变革》

研究方法

除了引言和结语两个部分，《领导变革》遵循简洁平实的行文方式：逐一介绍变革步骤，并用鲜活的事例和一般性讨论对各步骤进行详细阐述。这本书以直截了当的撰写方式，陈述较为通俗易懂的思想。科特用例灵活，这令他的思想方法受到管理者的青睐。事实上，书中的许多事例旨在为读者提供相关的参照点。下面试以一家饱受销售不力问题困扰的大型全球化制药公司的会议为例："如果有机会参加一次该公司典型的管理层会议，你会开始怀疑，有关公司的总收入、营业额、股票价格、客户投诉、竞争格局、士气等方面的情况是否真实。……会议氛围常常显得轻松、悠闲，讨论的是一些无关痛痒的问题。"[4] 阅读科特列举的事例，读者大都会感同身受，不由自主地移情于这些充满了自满情绪的组织情景中。列举此类事例，目的在于获得读者信任，贴近他们的实际经历。

时代贡献

《领导变革》沿用科特原创文章中提出的框架，但分析更详尽，用例更丰富。此前，科特出版了诸多有关组织变革和领导力的著作，《领导变革》的核心思想即可追溯到这些较早著作，例如《变革的力量：领导力与管理的差异》和《企业文化与业绩》。上述两部及后来出版的《新规则》[5]都蕴含了与《领导变革》相似的思想，并且仍在印行。从某种程度上说，要了解科特的思想是如何演进的，最佳的参照点就是其之前关于变革和转型的著述。

早期探索变革管理方面的著作焦点落在管理层行动等方面，而非循序渐进的变革过程。有两个典型的例子：克里斯·阿吉里斯的著述考察高层管理者如何应对不利局面；道格拉斯·麦格雷戈的《企业的人性面》阐明了什么因素和力量能够创造良好的工作环境，从而提升员工的业绩。[6]这些著作为科特的著作提供了思想基础，但是《领导变革》独具创意，游离于有关变革的学术研究传统之外。

---

1. 约翰·P.科特："领导变革：转型为何失败"，《哈佛商业评论》第73卷，1995年第2期，第59—67页。

2. 约翰·P.科特：《领导变革》，波士顿：哈佛商学院出版社，1996年，第 ix 页。

3. 科特：《领导变革》，第 ix 页。

4. 科特：《领导变革》，第37页。

5. 约翰·P.科特：《变革的力量：领导力与管理的差异》，纽约：自由出版社，1990年；约翰·P.科特、詹姆斯·L.赫斯克特：《企业文化与业绩》，纽约：自由出版社，1992年；约翰·P.科特：《新规则：21世纪企业和个人成功的八项理念》，纽约：自由出版社，1997年。

6. 克里斯·阿吉里斯：《国际竞争力与组织效益》，伊利诺伊州霍姆伍德：多尔西出版社，1962年；克里斯·阿吉里斯：《组织与创新》，伊利诺伊州霍姆伍德：R.D.欧文出版社，1965年；道格拉斯·麦格雷戈和乔·卡彻-格尔圣菲尔德：《企业的人性面》，纽约：麦格劳-希尔出版社，2006年。

第二部分：学术思想

5 思想主脉

要点 ⎤—

- 《领导变革》重点讨论商业组织如何演进及全球化的兴起。
- 科特列出了组织力图变革过程中常犯的八个错误，并提出了八个步骤的变革模式。
- 科特平实地陈述其观点，力避行业术语，善用鲜活事例。

核心主题

约翰·P.科特的《领导变革》一书紧紧围绕商业组织如何演进与转型这一主题展开。"变革"一词贯穿全书，其内涵丰富。科特预想了一家企业被迫"降低成本，提升产品和服务质量，寻求新的增长机会并提高生产率"，这些都是变革的例子——而这一清单可能并不完整。[1] 科特将变革与为了应对外部商业环境变化而引入的新商业实践相关联。重要的是，科特的变革模式适用性强，可用于公司面临的任何变革或挑战，无论是会计上的变动还是制造工序的革新。这一变革模式同样适用于制药公司、石油公司和综合性大学。

与上述主题密切相关的另一主题是全球化浪潮下变革的必要性——贸易条例*和运输成本的变化导致市场扩张，远远超出其物理边界。在科特看来，全球化是书中所论的诸多变革的动因。正如科特所言："经济全球化为所有人都创造了更多的机会，迫使公司进行大规模改进，这不仅是为了竞争与繁荣，更是为了生存。"[2] 换言之，在全球化浪潮之前，变革尚属锦上添花之举，而在全球化兴起之后，变革则是生死攸关的大事了。

> "从某种程度上讲，变革会带来相应的负面影响，这是不可避免的。当人类社会不得不改变自己以适应环境变化，痛苦必将相伴而生。但是，在过去十年的变革历程中，我们所目睹的巨大浪费和痛苦，其中绝大部分是可以避免的。"
>
> ——约翰·P.科特：《领导变革》

思想探究

《领导变革》专注于组织变革这一核心主题，为管理者提供实施变革的路线图。全书分为两大部分进行阐述：其一，罗列管理者通常犯的错误；其二，描述变革过程的八个步骤。

基于对企业变革计划的分析，科特列举出管理者在实施变革中通常所犯的八个错误：

1. 组织在推行变革的过程中未能激发员工的紧迫感，换言之，"过于容许自满情绪"。[3] 如果员工认为不需要改变其行为，他们将无法体会到组织处境的严峻性，也不会推动变革的进程。

2. 管理者未能创建由组织核心成员组成的领导联盟。在缺乏强有力的联盟领导的情况下，变革可能会持续一段时间，但"抗衡力量迟早会破坏这些计划"。[4]

3. 缺乏明智的愿景。

4. 沟通错误、沟通不足或缺乏沟通。

5. 未能创造有利环境。有时候，组织未能实现变革的障碍就在于过度僵化的"组织结构"，包括"主管拒绝顺应新环境"。[5]

6. 未能取得短期成效，比如运用小修小补的"节省成本法"（小型改革）或局部实施新生产方法，这样的短期成效可以助推整个变革项目。[6]

7. 在变革进程结束之前即宣告胜利。

8. 新行为未能深植于企业文化，致使变革未能充分扎根于企业以取得持续成功。[7]

对于此类问题，科特提出的解决方案是遵循变革的八个步骤。管理者可以同时执行多个步骤，但科特提醒，忽略任何一个步骤或对其未给予足够重视，变革进程就不会"以顺其自然、水到渠成的方式开展"，从而受阻。[8]变革过程的具体步骤如下：

1. 树立紧迫感。

2. 组建领导联盟。

3. 制定愿景与战略。

4. 传达变革愿景。

5. 全面授权赋能。

6. 创造短期成效。

7. 巩固成果并深化改革。

8. 将新途径深植于企业文化中。[9]

《领导变革》分章详细分析实施变革的每个步骤，并用许多公司的鲜活事例作为实施变革的说明。例如，在第三个步骤中，愿景指"一幅未来的图景，以隐含或明示的方式展现人们应为这样的未来而努力的理由"。[10]为了说明愿景的重要性，科特以一家"中型零售公司"作为一个实例。这家公司的总经理推出了一项颇具前景的计划，但有人认为其"含糊不清、软弱无力"。[11]尽管存在此种异议，总经理仍然成功地实现了他的愿景，这完全有赖于变革过程的前两个步骤：组建领导联盟和树立紧迫感。

语言表述

科特的文风简洁朴实、通俗易懂，没有学究气，书中善于运用实例来说明观点。这些实例的安排与内容对表述他的思想极为重要。例如，在关于自满情绪的一章中，科特采用了"一家大型全球化制药公司"的案例研究，这家公司"在过去几年中饱受困扰"。[12] 在与员工交谈的过程中，科特了解到，员工虽意识到问题之所在，但"缺乏高度的干劲"。[13] 这些实例来自鲜活的现实，运用恰到好处，使作者的主张更具说服力，也更切合现实。

《领导变革》通篇力避商业和经济行业术语，即使是管理经验有限或对企业文化知之甚少的读者，也能轻松把握变革的八个步骤。科特使用诸如"短期成效"、"企业文化"和"新愿景"等商业语言呈现其学术思想，读者无需具备专业知识，这令该书广为传播、受众广泛。

---

1. 约翰·P.科特：《领导变革》，波士顿：哈佛商学院出版社，1996 年，第 3 页。
2. 科特：《领导变革》，第 18 页。
3. 科特：《领导变革》，第 4 页。
4. 科特：《领导变革》，第 6 页。
5. 科特：《领导变革》，第 10 页。
6. 科特：《领导变革》，第 12 页。

7. 科特：《领导变革》，第 4—15 页。

8. 科特：《领导变革》，第 24 页。

9. 科特：《领导变革》，第 20—22 页。

10. 科特：《领导变革》，第 68 页。

11. 科特：《领导变革》，第 80 页。

12. 科特：《领导变革》，第 36 页。

13. 科特：《领导变革》，第 36 页。

6 思想支脉

要点 ⚷

- 科特的次要思想包括：领导力与管理的区别、未来组织的特征以及终身学习者的特征。

- 科特强调未来组织增强紧迫感并消除自满情绪的重要性。

- 科特将全球化视为一种即将到来的外力，但在当下，全球化已成为商业活动的既定事实，不再是举足轻重的要素。

其他思想

约翰·P.科特的《领导变革》中一个重要的次要观点是领导力在实施变革中的作用和重要性。科特对管理与领导力进行了区分，认为管理者必须具备领导特质，才能引领公司成功变革和转型。科特将管理与停滞懒散的官僚制度相联系，将有效的领导力与转型组织 * 相联系。"由于重点放在管理而非领导力上，官僚制度和关注内部管控的做法就占了上风。但是，随着公司因占据市场主导地位而持续取得成功，这一问题也常得不到解决，一种不良的自满情绪就开始滋生，所有这些因素致使转型更难以实现。"[1]

科特没有完全否定管理技能的作用，他指出诸如规划、预算、组织、人事、问题解决等重要事项必须得到有效的管理。相比之下，领导力是一个促进变革的过程，帮助组织在特定环境中确立和适应重大的变革。根据科特的观点："成功的转型需要 70%—90% 的领导力加 10%—30% 的管理。"[2]

另外两个次要观点是"未来组织"的特征以及如何在全球化经

济中培养杰出领导者的品格。[3]科特主张，由于商业环境的快速变化日益重要，组织务必继续做好以下工作：保持很强的紧迫感、拥有高效的领导联盟、善于沟通愿景、全面授权赋能、善于改变公司文化。科特进一步分析了未来的理想型高管。在科特看来，也许最重要的是，未来的领袖务必"终身学习"。

> "人们通常将重大转型与某一位具有较高知名度的大人物联系起来……这种想法非常危险。"
>
> —— 约翰·P. 科特：《领导变革》

思想探究

科特在论及"领导力比管理更为重要"这一观点时认为，问题的根源不在于变革管理，而在于管理者不具备出色的领导力品质。传统意义上的管理者创造的是"管理过度而领导力不足"的企业文化，官僚作风、骄傲自大、褊狭保守等情况严重。[4]科特认为，与其连根拔掉管理层，不如遴选和培育具有领导力潜能的管理者。

在书的最后几章中，科特展望了未来。在"未来的组织"一章中，他描述了他心目中未来成功管理的关键要素，并假设商业环境变化速度继续加快。科特写道，未来的组织应具备的最重要的特征之一就是"持续的紧迫感"。他如是说："高度的紧迫感并非意味着总是慌乱、焦虑或害怕，而是指一种消灭了自满情绪的状态；在此情形下，人们总是试图发现问题和寻找机会，其常规行为是'现在就行动'。"[5]这种紧迫感与"全面授权赋能"密切关联，后者是科特所预测的另一个步骤。基于几家技术公司成功创造赋权文化的实例，科特指出，在成功应对高水平变革的组织中，我们会看到以下特点："极为扁平的层级体系，几乎没有官僚作风，勇于承担风险的精神，全体员工大都各司其职，高层管理者集中负责领导。"[6] 换言之，在未来的成功组织里，干预式管理将被授权员工所取代，高层则集中负责领导。

为了确保组织找到合适人选任职，科特勾勒了未来的理想领导者：终身学习者。根据科特的观点，终身学习者具备五个特点：勇于冒险、如实评估自我、积极征求意见、善于倾听及开明接受新思想。[7] 他主张，与时俱进、继续学习比在某一时刻出人头地更加重要。[8]

被忽视之处

《领导变革》的核心思想直白明了，因此读者几乎不会忽略什么。理所当然地，变革的八个步骤使这本书广为流传，但读者较少关注到科特的次要思想。在八个步骤论述之外的另两章里，科特展望了未来组织与未来领导者，他十分谨慎地对待读者的期望。科特说："预测未来总是危险的，但本书讨论的内容具有相当明晰的意蕴。"[9] 科特论述不够充分的观点，较少在读者群中流传与分享。但是，科特核心思想的陈述条分缕析，犹如脱离于本书的独立实体，十分便于分享。

诚然，《领导变革》所述的全球化，就现在而言，其重要性已日渐式微。20 世纪 90 年代著书之时，全球化市场的前景是相对较新的议题；而在 21 世纪，这已成为普遍的事实。因此，当下的管理层不太会墨守科特的理念，继续强调全球市场带来的诸多挑战。全球化现在已成为既定的现实，而不是一种必须给予特别思考或准备的新兴现象。

1. 约翰·P.科特:《领导变革》, 波士顿: 哈佛商学院出版社, 1996 年, 第 27 页。

2. 科特:《领导变革》, 第 26 页。

3. 科特:《领导变革》, 第 161 页。

4. 科特:《领导变革》, 第 43 页。

5. 科特:《领导变革》, 第 162 页。

6. 科特:《领导变革》, 第 167 页。

7. 科特:《领导变革》, 第 183 页。

8. 科特:《领导变革》, 第 181 页。

9. 科特:《领导变革》, 第 162 页。

7 历史成就

要点 🗝

- 在《领导变革》中，约翰·P.科特成功地拓展了其关于企业变革如何达到最佳效果的思想。

- 这本书对商业之外的领域也颇具价值，惠及战争研究、卫生服务研究等领域。

- 《领导变革》的关注点是纯粹美式的。该书若能从更广泛的文化和地域视角展开论述，将更富成效。

观点评价

约翰·P.科特撰写《领导变革》一书，旨在拓展其早期同名文章中所陈述的思想，在这一点上，他是成功的。尽管20世纪90年代学界提出了其他的变革模式，但科特的变革模式的独创性在于其重点落在变革的过程上，且文风切近实际。学界在讨论变革之时，学究式理论色彩较浓，与之相比，科特密切关注商界，所引实例使其模式读起来更引人入胜。

科特的变革模式虽影响巨大，但并不具普遍性，因为他在书中所引的实例全部来源于西方国家。事实上，发展中国家和贫穷国家的组织要面对更加动荡多变的环境，更易受自然灾害以及政治环境、技术环境等不确定因素的影响。催生变革的背景、环境及宏观经济*环境与西方世界不同，需要不同的框架来指导变革管理。

科特著书之时考虑到了另一个重要的环境因素：北美自由贸

易协定 (NAFTA)* 1994 年 1 月 1 日正式生效，美国、加拿大与墨西哥之间实现自由贸易。这意味着，公司面临日益激烈的竞争和更大的挑战，因而必须对其商务流程进行变革和转型，以维护其市场份额。北美自由贸易协定很有可能是推动《领导变革》风行于世的因素之一，因为管理者不得不为更加一体化的世界经济预先规划。

> "与 20 年前相比，当今商业环境让我印象颇深的就是，成效（以及专门用来取得成效的手段）已成为大规模可持续变革的动力，其重要性日益显现。它们所产生的能量可以压倒各种阻碍变革的因素，包括急于求成、精力分散、劳动力稀释等不良效应。它们能助力打破阻碍变革的壁垒，因而也能化解全球化的复杂性，而全球化愈发让人感觉就像一场高速的 3D 国际象棋游戏。"
>
> —— 葛雷格·雷斯特 *："科特的变革八步骤是如何变化的？"

当时的成就

《领导变革》不仅获得了商业与管理界的广泛好评与高度认可，而且受到其他社会科学领域学者和从业者的青睐。变革的八个步骤模式成为各行业管理者的路线图，且被应用于战争研究、卫生服务研究、信息技术管理、劳资关系等领域。大学围绕这个模式设计了案例教学，用于教授学生如何实现领导变革项目。对研究人员和学者而言，这本书极具学术应用价值。例如，卫生服务研究使用科特的框架对英国国家层面的卫生服务进行了改革；信息技术管理专家运用该模式解释组织对新技术的引进，将员工对新结构、新工艺和新设备的抵抗情绪降至最低。

　　尽管《领导变革》以私营企业和大公司的案例为论述基础，其变革模式也被广泛用于解释卫生服务和教育等社会公益部门的变革和公共服务改革。变革八步骤模式还被应用于社会科学的各个领域，可见其超强适用性。这本书应用面之广也许出乎科特的意料，因为这本书最初是为企业高层管理人员和专业人员而写的。

　　《领导变革》在管理发展培训中也有一席之地。在组织中进行培训，其目的就是提供一种发展机会。科特的变革模式强调循序渐进、步骤明晰，以高层管理人员为目标读者，因此可作为一种卓越的工具，用于分析各种复杂形势。

局限性

　　科特所描述的是一般性的变革过程，适用于大部分的变革情形。这本书最大的局限之处在于：没有吸收发展中国家的实例。科特的用例主要源自他在北美组织工作的观察和体验，他所论及的公司事例绝大部分源自同一个国家：美国。他的八步骤框架确实具有广泛使用性，其步骤和论点理所当然地具有普遍性。尽管如此，管理者在开展组织分析时，也不应忽视内外部环境因素。

　　对变革情境方面的分析是这本书的另一不足之处。组织变革和转型已不再是 20 世纪 90 年代中期的"一次性"活动。当下，变革和转型具有更为持久的特性，因为公司要不断变革和转型，以保持竞争优势。情境（尤其是地理情境）的重要性不容忽视，但是科特没有关注国别差异。现在，变革不仅发生在美国或北美地区；随着商业全球化，各组织必须预测和回应世界范围内发生的变化，齐心协力，联合管理。科特若能开展比较分析，将世界其他区域的事例纳入其中，便可大幅优化其原有的分析。

8 著作地位

要点 🔑

- 在职业生涯中，科特以学者和管理顾问的双重身份，坚持不懈地投身于组织变革项目的分析与实施。

- 科特将自己的职业生涯分为两个阶段：第一阶段着重"研究"，第二阶段着重"实施"。

- 《领导变革》是科特最具影响力的著作之一，但在这部著作 1996 年面世之前，他已享有盛誉。

定位

约翰·P. 科特著《领导变革》之时，已出版了一些论述变革和领导力的文章与著作。1979 年，科特与合著者伦纳德·施莱辛格 * 发表"变革策略的选择"一文，介绍了后来在《领导变革》中论述的诸多思想。他们强调，要充分认识"人们对变革的有限容忍度"[1]，这是一个关键的变革阻力因素。这一观察与《领导变革》中描述的紧迫感紧密关联。在 1990 年出版的《变革的力量：领导力与管理的差异》一书中，科特主要关注有效领导力在变革中的作用。《领导变革》的重要思想——管理与领导力之间的差异也贯穿于《变革的力量》全书："领导力与管理的差异在于它们的主要职能，前者能产生有用的变革，后者能产生有序的结果来维持高效的工作。"[2]

然而，触发《领导变革》写作灵感最直接的根源是科特 1995 年发表的文章"领导变革：转型为何失败？"。[3] 这篇文章为科特构建实施变革的八个步骤提供了初始样本。《领导变革》面世以来，科特在数部作品中不断升华其变革思想，其中最为著名的是 2006 年出版的《冰山在融化》。这本书讲述一群企鹅被困于正在融化的冰山上的故事，显示了建立紧迫感以自救的重要性。同样，这个主题也是《领导变革》和科特早期作品的重要议题。

> "我过去所有的工作乃至现在的项目，在这跨越了几十年的研究中，我都运用了相同的公式。找出代表最成功的前 10% 或 20% 的案例，观察他们采取了什么行动，与身处那些情境中的人们交谈。然后，以上述同样的方式对普通或落后的案例进行调研，找出显示这些差距的模式是什么。报告这些因素并重点描述那些可以改变的因素，旨在将平均绩效提升到高绩效层次，或将滞后的绩效至少提升到标准水平。"
>
> ——约翰·P.科特：《变革加速器：构建灵活的战略以适应快速变化的世界》

整合

科特将其职业生涯分为两个阶段：第一阶段为 1972 年至 2008 年的研究阶段，第二阶段为 2008 年至今的实施阶段。[4] 研究阶段主要是发展了《领导变革》中详细阐述的变革的八个步骤。这一阶段科特的著作几乎全都是有关企业在转型期的行为。因此，其著作涵盖了领导力、管理、风险承担及组织行为等主题。变革管理这一主题贯穿于他们的所有著述，当然，有时仅在背景介绍的层面论及。

科特职业生涯的实施阶段主要指其在科特国际所从事的工作。

科特国际是科特于 2008 年联合创办的咨询公司，其使命宣言紧扣科特的研究主题，尤其是《领导变革》中所论述的主题。变革的八个步骤是科特国际网站上的重要内容。例如，该网站有一篇由葛雷格·雷斯特撰写的博客文章，名为"你的组织正在培养的是变革管理者还是变革领导者？"。雷斯特强调管理与领导力之间的差异："变革管理者与变革领导者的区别——如上述定义所示——不言而喻，非常重要。变革管理者通常驱动渐进的变革，确保工作在预算内按时完成；而变革领导者则不那么反对'混乱'，并敢于承担风险，能实施有影响力的激励措施，以推动大规模转型。"[5] 科特国际网站与《领导变革》同声共气、相互呼应，这表明科特职业生涯中的多种著作在理念上高度一致。

意义

《领导变革》是科特最具影响力的著作之一。科特国际网站强调了这本书的重要性："40 年来，哈佛商学院的科特教授致力于广泛而深入的研究，考察为何 70% 的商业组织未能成功实施他们的变革战略，而仅有 5% 的组织实现或超预期实现变革目标……科特的主要成就在于他 1996 年构建了领导变革的八个步骤，并荣获多个奖项。"[6]《领导变革》也是科特最畅销的作品之一，2011 年被《时代》周刊评为 25 本最具影响力的管理书籍之一。[7]

《领导变革》在科特的主要著作中依然占有一席之地，但要说他所赢得的名声有赖于这本书，就显得有些夸大其词。在这本书出版之前，他已经是商界学者中公认的佼佼者，在哈佛商学院担任重要职位长达 20 余年之久。再者，《领导变革》绝不是科特最具学术性或最严谨的著作；这本书没有脚注，也没有参考文献可循。我们可将这本书视为 20 世纪 90 年代中期科特思想升华的结晶，以及他构建后续著作的重要基础。

---

1. 约翰·P. 科特、伦纳德·施莱辛格："变革策略的选择"，《哈佛商业评论》（2008 年再版），登录日期 2015 年 5 月 21 日，https://hbr.org/2008/07/choosing-strategies-for-change/ar/1。

2. 约翰·P. 科特：《变革的力量：领导力与管理的差异》，纽约：自由出版社，1990 年，第 7 页。

3. 约翰·P. 科特："领导变革：转型为何失败？"，《哈佛商业评论》第 73 卷，1995 年第 2 期，第 59—67 页。

4. "关于我们"，科特国际，登录日期 2015 年 5 月 21 日，http://www.kotterinternational.com/about-us/。

5. 葛雷格·雷斯特："你的组织正在培养的是变革管理者还是变革领导者？"，登录日期 2015 年 5 月 21 日，http://www.kotterinternational.com/insights/organization-developing-change-managers-change-leaders/。

6. 科特国际："关于我们"。

7. "25 本最具影响力的商业管理书籍"，《时代》，2011 年 8 月 9 日，登录日期 2015 年 5 月 21 日，http://content.time.com/time/specials/packages/article/0,28804,2086680_2086683_2087679,00.html。

第三部分：学术影响

9 最初反响

要点 🔑

- 《领导变革》因过于僵化刻板及强调自上而下的领导力而备受学界批评。

- 虽然科特与评论家交流甚少，但 2012 年他对变革模式做了较大的修改，以适用于更加复杂多变的商业环境。

- 《领导变革》的评论家注意到，商业世界飞速变化，要求科特的模式随之改变。

批评

针对约翰·P. 科特《领导变革》一书的批评，其中一点是：由于变革过程复杂多变，没有任何单一模式能完全奏效。这本书极受读者欢迎；那么，如果书中的变革模式是正确的，大组织实现变革项目的成功率应获得显著提升，但事实似乎并非如此。正如卡洛琳·艾肯和斯科特·凯勒所言："科特的研究揭示了仅有 30% 的变革方案是成功的。自该书发行以来，成千上万的书和期刊论文开始关注这一主题，变革管理现已被纳入许多 MBA（工商管理硕士）*的专业课程。然而，2008 年麦肯锡*对全球 3 199 名总经理的调查报告发现，仅有三分之一转型成功，这一结果与科特的观点一致。过去 10 年的其他研究结论也与此惊人地相似。看来，尽管变革管理领域著作众多，但仍未能催生出较为成功的变革方案。"[1]

为此，艾肯和凯勒指出，变革管理实践"需要转型，提高对人们如何解读环境并选择行动的认识。"[2] 换言之，诸如科特那样的僵化刻板的模式，其产生的变革效果非常有限。

对《领导变革》的另一批评是：科特将变革描述为自上而下的实践。在 2009 年发表的"将公司作为社区重塑"一文中，加拿大管理学家亨利·明茨伯格＊承认，"科特的方法似乎足够合理，且可能富有成效。"但他质疑主要由一位"高层领导者"来推动变革的观点。他写道："要重塑公司的话，可能不应采用自上而下或自下而上的方法，而应采用两者的折中方法，从中层出发，将各个部门的中层管理者团结起来，形成组织变革的中坚力量。"[3] 虽然科特提及要为员工创造短期成效，但自上而下的变革会导致员工的挫败感。进而言之，科特的模式是循序渐进、分阶段实现变革的过程，未能考虑到诸多意料之外的问题，而这些问题必须得到妥善处理，才能确保变革项目获得成功。

一些作者质疑科特关于管理和领导力方面的观点。管理学理论家加里·尤克尔＊认为，领导力是管理任务的一部分，组织中每一位管理者都应承担起这一任务，要成功经营组织和实施转型，领导力和管理技能同等重要。[4]

> "尽管对于组织变革管理模式众说纷纭，难以达成一致，但就两大重要问题似乎已有共识：第一，当前商业环境下，变革步伐之快前所未有……第二，由内外因素引起的变革，其形式多样、规模不一。"
>
> —— 卢恩·托尼姆·拜：《组织变革管理的评论》

回应

尽管科特已对《领导变革》中的八步骤模式作了修订，但他仍极少与评论家公开交流。2012 年，他在《哈佛商业评论》发表了题为"变革加速器"一文，[5] 用"战略系统"代替变革的八步骤模式："这个系统拓展了我 15 年前提出的八步骤模式。"[6] 变革的"战略模式"与"八步骤模式"有三大不同之处。第一，变革的八步骤模式"操作起来往往僵化刻板，十分有限，且需循序渐进"，然而，战略模式关注到加速变革的因素，"这些因素同时存在并总起着作用。"[7] 这一改良模式也许由不断变化的商业环境所催生——由于变化在加速，显然，维持原有线性发展、分阶段实现的过程已不再可能。第二，八步骤模式的变革过程由一个"精干而强大的团队"引领和推动，而"加速器模式尽可能吸纳全组织的成员，组成一支变革'志愿军'。"[8] 第三，加速器模式的基础信念是，组织是与社会网络之间存在信息沟通的，而不是一个自上而下的结构。

科特没有引用批评家的观点，并以此作为其模式改良的灵感，但他参考了三位学者的著作，以引领模式改良的方向。哈佛商学院教授迈克尔·波特*让科特"恍然大悟：组织需要更加明确地、更加频繁地重视战略"。[9] 克莱顿·克里斯坦森*同样来自哈佛，他的著作向科特展示了在快节奏的环境中，组织是如何疲于应对技术变革管理。丹尼尔·卡尼曼*"将大脑分为两个互相配合的系统，一个更加感性，一个更加理性。"[10] 值得注意的是，这几位学者并非将组织变革作为主要研究方向。

冲突与共识

商业环境复杂多变，因此，没有一种绝对权威可靠的转型和变革模式。然而，该学科文献的一些趋势以及科特自己对模式的改良，意味着一定程度的共识仍然存在。共识的一方面在于，变革模

式必须吸收新的方法，比如社会网络分析*。这一方法可以更准确
地描绘信息如何在组织内传播，而不是像官方的公司结构所显示
的那样。这类研究工具在 1996 年仅有部分已获得开发，因此，科
特的著作中并没有运用这些新方法，这不足为奇。普遍共识的另一
方面是，组织变革不太可能像一系列事件那样展开，而是经历不断
的演变并常常处于无序的状态。正如莱安德罗·赫雷罗*2014 年在
《领导变革》的书评中所说："线性的、有序的世界已不复存在。"[11]
赫雷罗本欲以此作为对科特模式的批判，但科特本人已否定了其模
式的循序性特征。

　　围绕《领导变革》主题所达成的另一个共识是，转型已成为当
今商业环境中不可或缺的要素，组织应投入资源，探索如何能最有
效地实现转型。科特 1996 年伏案写作之时不得不花大量的时间说
服读者，全球化管理需要更关注变革项目。由于全球化已完全融入
商业环境，现已无需为此再大费周章。

---

1. 卡洛琳·艾肯和斯科特·凯勒："变革管理的非理性面"，2009 年 4 月，登录日期 2015 年 5 月 21 日，http://www.mckinsey.com/insights/organization/the_irrational_side_of_change_management。

2. 艾肯和凯勒："变革管理的非理性面"。

3. 亨利·明茨伯格："将公司作为社区重塑"，《哈佛商业评论》，2009 年 7 月，登录日期 2015 年 5 月 21 日，https://hbr.org/2009/07/rebuilding-companies-as-communities。

4. 加里·A. 尤克尔：《组织领导力》，新泽西州上鞍河：普伦蒂斯·霍尔出版社，2010 年。

5. 约翰·P. 科特："变革加速器"，《哈佛商业评论》，2012 年 11 月，登录日期 2015 年 5 月 21 日，https://hbr.org/2012/11/accelerate。

6. 科特："变革加速器"。

7. 科特："变革加速器"。

8. 科特："变革加速器"。

9. 科特："变革加速器"。

10. 科特："变革加速器"。

11. 莱安德罗·赫雷罗："约翰·科特八个步骤变革管理模式是上世纪最佳的变革模式，仍盛行于 2014 年的事实超出我的想象"，2014 年 10 月 21 日，登录日期 2015 年 5 月 21 日，http://leandroherrero.com/john-kotters-8-step-change-management-model-is-the-best-change-model-of-the-last-century-why-this-is-still-alive-in-2014-is-beyond-me/。

10 后续争议

要点 🔑

- 《领导变革》详述了组织变革过程最早的模式之一，启发了该领域的后续著作。

- 变革研究可按三种方式进行分类：第一类研究变革的发生率，第二类研究变革的发生方式，第三类研究变革的规模。《领导变革》属于第二类研究。

- 《领导变革》影响深远，并启发了诸如彼得·圣吉、杰弗里·莱克*和詹姆斯·弗兰兹*等学者的变革模式，他们的著作考察更广泛环境下的变革过程。

应用与问题

1996 年约翰·P.科特的《领导变革》初版之时，许多作者已将变革视为商业环境不可或缺的部分。随着时间推移，人们普遍认可变革应该成为组织战略的永恒主题，越来越多的学者开始构建各自的变革过程模式。考察变革的重要性及其实现途径的文献不断增长，但运用实验数据来验证相关理论模型的却极其少见。

《领导变革》成书之时，正值组织为了进行业务转型而实施流程再造*、全面质量管理*、组织重组和技术变革。科特的同名文章深受读者青睐，说明人们在思考组织的变革，但对取得最佳成效的路径不甚明了。这本书的出版标志着组织变革过程模式的开端：科特构建的模式使变革过程不再高深莫测，少了些不可预测性。他向读者展示了变革的结果是可预见的；而且，如果正确遵循模式顺序，组织可以实现成功的转型。

彼得·圣吉、杰弗里·K.莱克和詹姆斯·K.弗兰兹等后来者发展了科特的思想，使之能应用于更广泛的商业环境。他们的著作集中考察混乱无序、复杂多变环境下的组织变革，充分考虑权变因素*（未知的影响或事件）以及迫使组织变革和适应的内外环境。由于无法预先为这些力量作好准备，变革项目也就不能以渐进有序的方式实施。于是，这些作者提出了周期性*变革的观点。

> "在21世纪，如同组织要被迫学习、变革和不断自我创新一样，越来越多的个人也会这样做。科特继续强调，随着变革步伐加快，持续发展——或者说继续学习——的意愿和能力成为个人职业成功的关键，也是组织取得经济效益的关键。"
>
> ——加里·汤姆林森："约翰·P.科特《领导变革》书评"

思想流派

变革领域的文献可分为三大思想主流或学派：[1]

1. 变革的发生率。

2. 变革的发生方式。

3. 变革的规模。

科特的著作属于上述第二类学派，即通过考察变革的发生方式来探索变革。这一学派可以追溯至库尔特·M.勒温的论著。根据勒温的观点，成功的变革方案要经历三个阶段：解冻现有阶段、变革阶段（迈上一个新台阶）、再冻结阶段。[2] 这个模式提供了一个变革规划方案，强调要摒弃组织中陈旧的行为、结构、过程和文化。理查德·吕

克 *、伯纳德·伯恩斯 * 等知名作者也探索了变革规划方案，并构建了与勒温相似的模式。伯恩斯批评了"存在一套最佳变革战略"的说法，并指出每一个新模式仅意在用一套方案代替另一套方案。他认为，对于什么需要变革以及如何实施变革，组织均可自主选择。[3]

这一学派的作者大多提出了有计划性的、循序性的变革模式，这些模式与科特的模式相似。其中一些模式重视环境因素，并考虑以下权变因素：事情并非总按计划进行，有时根本不可能遵循计划行事。管理者要保持谨慎，以应对权变因素，并适时调整计划。在这一学派中，科特的变革模式成为所有后续变革模式的基准。这一领域后来取得的成果表明，科特的模式对于组织的变革与转型管理是一个良好的起点。

当前研究

当今，尽管研究重点已从探索作为步骤顺序的变革过程转向更宽泛地理解变革，但是组织变革仍是一个富有争议的讨论主题和学术领域。这个领域中的许多重要学者以科特的著述为起点继续前行，将新的研究系统应用于变革过程研究。科特的思想可能在他自己的咨询公司——科特国际——的成员著作中发挥得最为淋漓尽致。科特国际以与《领导变革》相似的构架和基调，定期发表关于变革的文章。例如，最近一篇由葛雷格·雷斯特撰写的文章追问："你的组织正在培养的是变革管理者还是变革领导者？"这篇文章要求读者在一组选项之间作出选择，诸如"我们把所有的项目都列入预算"或者"我们正在积极调动资源"，以确定他们的组织正在培养的是变革领导者还是变革管理者。[4] 这一区分首次出现在《领导变革》中，而且仍然是科特理论框架的重要组成部分。

另一篇文章讨论了领导力是否可以传授的问题："犹如科特教授所经常论及的，最有效的领导者知道如何、何时与人拉近距离、凝聚人心：一切的关键在于平衡。由于变革已成为一天、一年甚至一个时代的常态，领导力就变得无比重要了。"[5] 还有一篇文章分析了奥巴马总统*的案例。他参加网络脱口秀节目"两蕨之间"，以推广 2010 年美国平价医疗法案*的医疗服务改革。此文作者将该事件与成功交际者的技巧联系起来——这也正是《领导变革》的重要主题——并作了这样的结论："优秀的交际者必须乐意在他们的舒适区之外发表讲话。"[6]

---

1. 卢恩·托尼姆·拜："组织变革管理的评论"，《变革管理杂志》第 5 卷，2005 年，第 369—380 页。

2. 库尔特·勒温："群体动力学前沿 II：群体生活的渠道；社会规划与行动研究"，《人际关系》第 1 卷，1947 年，第 143—153 页。

3. 理查德·吕克：《管理变革与转型》，波士顿：哈佛商学院出版社，2003 年；伯纳德·伯恩斯："无这种管理组织变革的'最佳方式'"，《管理决策》第 34 卷，1996 年第 10 期，第 11—18 页。

4. 葛雷格·雷斯特："你的组织正在培养的是变革管理者还是变革领导者？"，登录日期 2015 年 5 月 21 日，http://www.kotterinternational.com/insights/organization-developing-change-managers-change-leaders/。

5. 葛雷格·雷斯特："领导力可以传授吗？"，登录日期 2015 年 5 月 21 日，http://www.kotterinternational.com/insights/can-leadership-be-taught/。

6. 肖恩·斯皮尔蒙："为何'两蕨之间'是奥巴马的医疗卫生服务法案的秘密武器"，登录日期 2015 年 5 月 21 日，http:// www.kotterinternational.com/insights/two-ferns-obamas-health-care-secret-weapon/。

11 当代印迹

要点 🗝

• 《领导变革》是变革管理领域的经典之作，在当下依旧具有一定影响力。

• 线性变革模式与复合变革模式之间有何差异？两种模式孰利孰弊？争论仍在继续。

• 一些批评者认为科特的模式僵化刻板，他们认为常识和灵活性比规定性的步骤更重要。

地位

约翰·P.科特的《领导变革》是变革管理领域的经典之作，在当下仍具有一定影响力。然而，这本书所产生的重要影响大都是通过科特随后的工作来实现的，这些工作细化和修正了变革的八个步骤模式。

组织转型没有单一的公式，但遵循一个计划好的方案，比如科特的八个步骤框架，可以提高组织转型的成功率。彼得·诺斯豪斯*在他的论述领导力理论的著作中承认，领导力对于催生变革是举足轻重的，他认为管理和领导力不仅相辅相成，而且对成功的管理者而言不可或缺。[1]这些后续的相关著作彰显了《领导变革》一书的价值所在。

在过去二三十年中，变革与转型深深影响了各行业组织。孕育于20世纪90年代的组织变革与转型这一概念，其意蕴在当今无甚变化。但是，组织变革和转型已变得愈加复杂。尽管学界探索组织变革与转型已长达 20 余年，但变革往往依然是"反应性的、非连续性的和临时性的，所有已启动实施的变革方案中约有 70% 宣告失败。"[2] 当前的争论主题仍然是寻求合适有效的组织变革管理框架。尽管许多学者提出了各自的变革框架，但上述数据显示，我们仍需做更多的工作。科特的《领导变革》将继续在此类研究中扮演重要角色。

> "世界上差不多所有的组织都会经历一个非常相似的生命周期。它们始于网状结构，有点像一个有太阳、行星、卫星甚至人造卫星的太阳系。创始人处在中心位置，其他人在不同的节点工作，承担不同的职能。行动就是寻求机会并承担风险，并以人们相信的愿景为导向……随着时间的推移，一个成功的组织经历一系列阶段的演变……成为一个有层次结构、由众所周知的管理过程所驱动的企业。"
>
> ——约翰·P.科特：《变革加速器：构建灵活的战略以适应快速变化的世界》

互动

《领导变革》的思想并不直接与当代学者或思想流派的观点相抵触，但它确实将作者早期的观点和作品融于一体，强调领导力和将变革视为一个过程的重要性。在过去的 20 年里，这个领域有大量相关的研究；线性变革模式和复合变革模式之间仍存相异之处。线性变革模式认为变革是一个分阶段的过程——假若公司的管理者按顺序执行每个步骤，就能成功实施变革方案。相比之下，复合变革模式则将变革描述为持续性的、非线性的过程。

尽管此项研究和诸多论文、著作致力于变革管理研究，但是大多数变革方案仍无法取得预期的理想效果。[3]这对提出变革模式（尤其是已付诸实施的模式，如科特模式）的理论家来说是一种挑战。对这些模式进行回顾并提出新的变革和转型理论的时机已经成熟。马尔科姆·希格斯 * 和黛博拉·罗兰 * 2005 年刊发的文章指出，[4]实际上，与线性变革模式（例如科特、迈克尔·哈默 * 和詹姆斯·钱皮 * 的模式[5]）相比，复合变革模式（例如彼得·圣吉、杰弗里·K. 莱克和詹姆斯·K. 弗兰兹的模式[6]）已被证明更为有效。

持续争议

关于变革的文献呈现出多样化的研究和争论领域。科特已经修改了其变革模式，以适应当前的商业环境，且基于最新的行为科学研究成果，引入了更灵活的方法。一些作者仍然质疑科特最初的变革模式。咨询专家莱安德鲁·赫雷罗曾批评科特仍在继续推广其刻板的、分阶段的变革模式，而世界的复杂性要求更大的灵活性。他写道："科特的变革步骤永远不会产生革命，无论是1996 年的模式还是 2014 年的模式。然而，'革命'可能不是行业改造的目标，因此科特的模式无可厚非。但是，要勇于抛弃它。对更宏大的管理而言，要品读科特的思想，心怀感恩，然后眺望窗外的世界，展望未来。"[7]

值得注意的是，这一最新的批评针对的是科特 2014 年重写的变革模式，而不是其 1996 年在《领导变革》中构建的模式。赫雷罗认为，科特新构建的非线性模式仍过于僵化刻板。他带有嘲讽意味地提及科特本人的建议，即管理者要"同时且连续地"执行这些步骤："欢迎来到 2014 年或 2015 年。正如其公司网站所说，'在广泛研究之后'，'同时且连续地执行步骤'用了 19 年才成为一条建议。以这种龟速才能做出发现，简直赶得上梵蒂冈了。"[8] 这样的批评是罕见的，但表达了另一种观点。由于科特的作品深受欢迎，而且声望很高，这种另类的观点可能并不多见。

---

1. 彼得·盖伊·诺斯豪斯：《领导力：理论与实践》，加利福尼亚州千橡市：塞奇出版社，2004 年。

2. 卢恩·托尼姆·拜："组织变革管理的评论"，《变革管理杂志》第 5 卷，2005年，第 378 页。

3. 马尔科姆·希格斯和黛博拉·罗兰："一切大小变革：探索变革方法及其领导力"，《变革管理杂志》第 5 卷，2005 年第 2 期，第 121—151 页；约翰·P. 科特：《变革的力量：领导力与管理的差异》，纽约：自由出版社，1990 年。

4. 希格斯和罗兰："一切大小变革：探索变革方法及其领导力"。

5. 彼得·M. 圣吉：《第五项修炼：学习型组织的艺术与实践》，伦敦：世纪商业出版社，1991 年；杰弗里·K. 莱克和詹姆斯·K. 弗兰兹：《丰田汽车精益模式的实践：结合战略和卓越经营以实现卓越绩效》，纽约：麦格劳－希尔出版社，2011 年。

6. 约翰·P. 科特：《领导变革》，波士顿：哈佛商学院出版社，1996 年；迈克尔·哈默和詹姆斯·钱皮：《企业再造：商业革命宣言》，纽约：哈珀商业出版社，1993 年。

7. 莱安德鲁·赫雷罗："变革管理：哈佛，你遇到难题"，登录日期 2015 年 5 月 21日，http://learndroherrero.com/change-management-harvard-you-have-a-problem/。

8. 赫雷罗："变革管理：哈佛，你遇到难题"。

12 未来展望

要点 ⚿

- 《领导变革》仍会是变革文献中的一部重要经典，但随着新方法不断加深我们对组织变革的理解，其重要性日渐式微。

- 哈佛商学院的朱莉·巴蒂拉娜*等学者通过扩大学习技术的范围，把重点放在员工而不是管理者上，继续将科特的思想向前推进。

- 《领导变革》是在变革成为一个新兴话题之时创作的。此书清晰易懂、内容全面、事例鲜活，因而成为变革领域的奠基之作。

潜力

约翰·P.科特的《领导变革》仍是组织变革领域的里程碑之作。与1996年相比，正确把握和实施变革在当下显得尤为重要。各工商企业每天要迎接新的挑战，必须紧跟最新的市场动向和技术革新。这迫使他们改变经营方法、企业文化、业务流程，以赶上全球化大潮的步伐，保持全球化竞争的优势。只要变革仍是商业活动的一个重要部分，《领导变革》中的原则就会继续发挥相应的作用。

《领导变革》的未来潜力与变革模式的发展息息相关，这些模式应能反映出未来组织的适应力。科特预测了灵活型企业的兴起，但商业结构的转型比他想象的更加迅猛。对《领导变革》的一种批评是，该模式过于关注组织的高层管理者。正如凯莉·奥基夫所言："变革八步骤模式给领导者和管理者施加巨大压力，但对员工无甚要求。对管理者的期望是，他们要会缓解恐惧，有解决所有问题的方法，成为专业的沟通者，并善于管理人才，而员工只需跟随效仿、按部就班即可。"[1] 通过整合来自实施变革第一线员工的反馈意见，或者通过更加注重不确定因素、员工参与变革的程度等方面，我们可以进一步完善科特的变革八步骤模式。

> "当然，正式授权是影响力的重要源泉。以往研究表明，对处于典型组织结构底层的人员而言，推动变革是很难做到的——一个典型的组织结构具备多个职能团队、明确的职位层级以及预先设定的汇报程序。但是，大多数学者和从业者也已认识到组织网络所产生的非正式影响的重要性。"
>
> —— 朱莉·巴蒂拉娜和蒂茨娅娜·卡希亚洛：
> 《大变革者的网络效应》

未来方向

哈佛商学院副教授朱莉·巴蒂拉娜或许是能将变革领导力研究朝这一方向推进的学者。巴蒂拉娜运用网络分析方法（即使用图论和网络模型来研究社会行为），以了解领导者如何在企业中实施重大变革。在《大变革者的网络秘密》一文中，巴蒂拉娜与其合著者蒂茨娅娜·卡希亚洛运用社会网络模型，研究了英国国家医疗服务体系 * 的68个改革计划。这一模型考察组织中的个体及其彼此之间的联系网络，以确定某一个体是否在推动变革、阻碍变革，或者对变革漠不关心。

基于网络分析方法，她们的研究发掘了科特模式所没有涵盖的变革领导力的三个方面。第一，"处于组织非正式网络核心位置的变革者，无论在正式层级中所处何种位置，都具有明显的优势。"[2] 换言之，即便没有正式权力，公司中与他人关系良好的个人对变革也是至关重要的。第二，能将分散的团体（很难联合的团体）联合起来的个人更善于实施重大变革，而拥有内聚性网络关系（将大多数或全部个体连接在一起）的个人更善于应对较小的变革。最后，保持与"中立者"的联系，即与"对变革摇摆不定"的个人保持联系，这对实施变革是十分有利的。相反，与抵触变革者保持联系则会降低变革的成功率。这项研究致力于实现《领导变革》的潜在目标：从个人层面理解变革工作如何在组织中贯彻实施。科特的领导联盟理念可由网络分析取而代之，因为网络分析能更严谨地考察联盟的运作方式及其成员的构成特征。

小结

《领导变革》一书自出版以来，在课堂教学和董事会中发挥了举足轻重的作用，成为各大型组织探索如何实施变革的主流视角之一。科特将切合实际的"八步骤模式"与众多实例有机结合，使这本书成为各个层级未来领导者的实用指南。20年来，这本书对管理者如何思考组织转型产生了深远的影响，而且其知识体系有利于培育学生在职场中更有效地与管理者沟通交流。

《领导变革》成书之时，各类组织才刚刚开始意识到组织变革的重要性。从那时起，变革已经成为商业环境中的一个永恒主题。科特以一种非常朴实、平易近人和通俗易懂的方式展示了他的研究成果。这本书辨析了管理者所犯的阻碍变革的常见错误：管理者品读此书之时，可以将这些错误与自身经历联系起来，找到彼此的相似之处。《领导变革》所展现的谈话式口吻是其写作特色，让不同水平的读者都能体会到，这本书不仅实用性强，而且趣味盎然。

1. 凯莉·奥基夫："科特八步骤出错之处",《行政首长博客》, 登录日期 2015 年 5
   月 21 日, https://www.executiveboard.com/blogs/where-kotters-8-steps-gets-it-wrong/。
2. 朱莉·巴蒂拉娜和蒂茨娅娜·卡希亚洛："大变革者的网络秘密",《哈佛商业
   评论》, 登录日期 2015 年 5 月 21 日, https://hbr.org/2013/07/the-network-secrets-of-
   great-change-agents/ar/1。

术语表

1. **平价医疗法案（也被称作"奥巴马医疗法案"）**：2010 年美国国会通过的法令，是自 1965 年以来美国医疗保障制度最重大的改革。这部法案要求美国人都拥有某种医疗保险，并建立保险交易所，以使保险市场具有竞争性。

2. **全面授权赋能**：广大员工在决策过程中的代表权和参与权。

3. **复合成长**：描述指数级增长或对数级增长的概念，即建立在自身上的成长；复合成长的原则意味着个人和职业两者的共同发展。

4. **权变因素**：影响规划和战略的商业环境因素，包括外部环境和技术变化。

5. **企业文化**：企业员工和管理层的共同价值观、信念和处事方式。企业文化决定了人们在企业内部的互动方式以及企业处理其业务和外部关系的方式。

6. **周期性变革**：一种变革领导力方法，强调不能将变革理解为分阶段的过程，并为领导者提供有关领导变革的新型指南。

7. **国内市场**：某个特定国家内部的商品和服务市场。

8. **经济学**：研究商品和服务的生产、分配和消费的一门社会科学。

9. **自由贸易**：一种不限制国家间贸易的政策，一般通过取消关税和其他贸易壁垒来实现。

10. **全球 5 000 家公司**：一个数据库，包含 5 000 家私营公司和公开招股公司的数据，这些公司来自数个行业，营收额超过 50 万亿美元。

11. **全球化**：一个使世界似乎变得越来越小的过程。在一般情况下彼此不接触的群体之间，随着通讯进步，逐步实现文化、商业、宗教

和政治等层面的日益沟通和扩大交流。

12. **领导联盟**：一个有权力、有动力推动和领导组织变革的群体。

13. **国际经济一体化**：指诸如关税及贸易总协定（GATT）等协定。关贸总协定是规范国际贸易的多边国际协定，其目的是为了各个国家之间的共同利益削减关税和其他贸易壁垒。关贸总协定签订于1947年，持续至1994年，随后由世界贸易组织（WTO）取代。

14. **领导力**：通常指一种品格或一组品格特征，包括远见、魅力、毅力、权力和智慧，并能转化为有效的社会变革执行力。领导力也可以是通过争取他人的支持来实现变革的过程。

15. **领导力研究**：一个多学科学术领域，目的是确定成功的领导力特征和理解组织中的领导力环境。

16. **学习型组织**：由彼得·圣吉及其麻省理工学院斯隆管理学院同事首创的一个术语，并用于圣吉《第五项修炼——学习型组织的艺术与实践》一书。这本书论及组织必备的五大修炼：系统思考、自我驾驭、心智模式、共同愿景和团队学习。学习型组织重视团队合作与合作管理模式。

17. **终身学习**：个人和职业不断成长与发展的过程。

18. **宏观经济学**：经济学的一个分支，研究经济增长、货币供应及技术的长期趋势等宏观经济因素。

19. **管理**：企业与组织中协调公司不同分支工作的职能。管理者通常要以最小的成本或努力来完成目标。

20. **目标管理法**：由彼得·德鲁克提出的一种管理方法，将结果与公司目标挂钩，这些目标又与管理行为相关联。

21. **管理咨询**：帮助公司提升业绩的过程，一般通过分析公司的业务流程和战略来实现。

22. **管理学**：致力于透视商业组织内部业务流程的一门学科，研究如何改进这些流程以实现最大化的商业目标。

23. **MBA（工商管理硕士）**：一种硕士学位，最初于 19 世纪末工业化初期在美国颁发，作为衡量工商领域学术水平的标准。

24. **麦肯锡**：指麦肯锡公司，一家跨国管理咨询公司，为企业提供分析报告，帮助企业做出正确的管理决策。

25. **英国国家医疗服务体系**：英国的公费医疗服务体系。

26. **北美自由贸易协定**：美国、加拿大及墨西哥于 1994 年 1 月签署生效的一个自由贸易协定，其目的是消除美、加、墨三国间的贸易壁垒。

27. **组织行为学**：关于组织中的个体与群体活动的研究。

28. **政治学**：研究政治制度和过程的社会科学。

29. **流程再造**：运用信息技术创新公司业务运营方式，以提高生产率，削减成本。

30. **短期成效**：阶段性成效，其目的可能是一个较大目标而不是最终目标。

31. **社会网络分析**：运用网络模型和图表，研究社会结构及其在其他机构的运作方式。

32. **技术变革**：指更快、更好的通讯（互联网革命），更好的交通工具，以及实现全球化沟通的信息网络。

33. **X 理论和 Y 理论**：由道格拉斯·麦格雷戈构建的组织行为模型，管理者运用 X 理论和 Y 理论去了解员工。基于 X 理论，员工被假定天生懒惰怠工，而 Y 理论则假定员工自我激励、进取心强。

34. **全面质量管理**：一套管理原则，要求每位公司成员在每个领域都必须保持用最高的标准工作，从而提升客户的满意度。

35. **贸易条例**：涵盖国际贸易分析和监管的法律领域，特别关注限制反竞争行为，例如不公平定价和垄断。

36. **转型组织**：在运作方式上进行重大变革的组织。转型可以指生产过程、招聘过程或组织的任何主要职能方面的变革。

人名表

1. **克里斯·阿吉里斯**（1923—2013），美国商业学者，研究组织结构与公司行为的关系，也关注行动科学的发展。行动科学研究人类面对挑战时如何设计行动方案。

2. **阿喀琉斯·A.阿米纳基斯**，美国商业学者，目前任教于奥本大学，主要研究方向为变革管理。

3. **朱莉·巴蒂拉娜**，法国商业学者，目前任教于哈佛商学院，其著作研究个人和组织如何摆脱根深蒂固的规范，以改变他们的行为方式。

4. **W.沃纳·伯克**，美国哥伦比亚大学教育学院的心理学和教育学教授，在哥伦比亚大学带领工作组研究伯克-利特文组织变革模式。

5. **伯纳德·伯恩斯**（1953年生），斯特林管理学院的组织变革教授，研究领域涉及运用不同的变革途径来提升或削弱组织中的伦理行为。

6. **詹姆斯·钱皮**（1942年生），管理顾问，组织变革、企业重组与复兴等管理问题的权威人物。

7. **克莱顿·克里斯坦森**（1952年生），哈佛商学院教授，被誉为创新与增长研究领域的顶级专家之一，其思想被广泛应用于世界范围的各类组织。

8. **威廉·爱德华兹·戴明**（1900—1993），美国工程师与管理顾问。他拥有丰富而广泛的履历，其学术贡献之一是在《走出困境》一书中提出的全面质量管理措施，书中论述了管理者应如何实现可持续的组织变革。

9. **彼得·德鲁克**（1909—2005），奥地利裔美国管理顾问和学者，现代管理学之父。他协助构建了现代企业实体的实践基础，以其提出的目标管理法而著称。

10. **尼尔斯·芬斯塔德**，组织变革领域的挪威学者，曾任职于博德地区大学。

11. 詹姆斯·K.弗兰兹，美国商人，丰田之道学院全球运营副总裁。

12. 蒂莫西·加尔平，美国科罗拉多州大学管理学教授；同时也是商业顾问，业务涉及战略规划、重组和组织变革等领域。

13. 迈克尔·哈默（1948—2008），美国作家和工程师，其企业流程再造管理法影响深远。

14. 希瑟·哈夫曼，美国加利福尼亚州大学伯克利分校组织理论教授，致力于研究面临内外环境变化的组织及其人员如何寻求发展。

15. 莱安德罗·赫雷罗，顾问、临床心理学家、讲师，查尔方特项目（监督病毒变化方案）首席执行官，致力于创新和实施大规模行为与文化变革。

16. 马尔科姆·希格斯，英国南安普顿商学院的人力资源管理和组织行为学教授，其学术方向包括变革管理，尤其是积极情绪与变革领导力的关系研究。

17. 阿诺德·S.贾德森，作家、管理顾问，出版变革项目领域的书籍，任波士顿贾德森战略管理咨询公司总裁。

18. 丹尼尔·卡尼曼（1934年生），以色列裔美国心理学家，普林斯顿大学伍德罗·威尔逊学院荣誉教授，诺贝尔经济学奖获得者。

19. 葛雷格·雷斯特（1965年生），科特国际执行副总裁，负责全球商业发展与客户业务。

20. 库尔特·M.勒温（1890—1947），德国裔美国心理学家，社会与组织心理学先驱，构建了分析影响社会现实因素的框架，即力场分析。后者被用于组织变革研究，以分析影响变革过程的相关因素。

21. 杰弗里·K.莱克，美国密歇根大学工业与运营工程教授，拥有莱克精益咨询公司。他的著作研究管理技术的成功运用，例如在丰田汽车公司中的运用。

22. 乔治·利特文，美国组织心理学家，曾在哈佛商学院任教，研究领域包括成功领导者素质。

23. 理查德·吕克（1943 年生），出版多部商业与管理领域的著作，包括《企业家工具包》（2004）和《忙碌经理业务委派指南》（2009）等。

24. 道格拉斯·麦格雷戈（1906—1964），管理学者，在麻省理工学院度过了其大部分职业生涯，最大贡献或许是将人类行为引入组织分析中。

25. 亨利·明茨伯格（1939 年生），加拿大学者和顾问，出版了《管理者，而非 MBA》《管理之简》等多部著作，研究重点是管理工作、战略制定和组织形式等领域。

26. 彼得·诺斯豪斯，美国西密歇根大学传播学院传播学荣誉教授，专注于领导力模式、领导力评估和群体动力学研究。

27. 贝拉克·奥巴马（1961 年生），第 44 任美国总统，是美国历史上第一位非裔美国人总统。他推行了数十年来的首次医疗保险方面的重大改革方案，即 2010 年的"患者保护与平价医疗法案"。

28. 迈克尔·波特（1947 年生），哈佛商学院教授，以提出"五种竞争力量"模式而著称。

29. 黛博拉·罗兰，无铅咨询公司创始人，该公司为企业提供变革管理咨询。她也是变革指南《保持行之有效的变革领导力》的合著者。

30. 伦纳德·施莱辛格，哈佛商学院教授，研究组织中有效领导者的角色。

31. 彼得·圣吉（1947 年生），美国系统科学家，现任教于麻省理工学院；最具影响力的著作是《第五项修炼》，该书详述了学习型组织理论。

32. 托马斯·沃尔曼（1937—2009），美国商业教授，制造控制系统领域的领军人物。

33. 加里·尤克尔（1940 年生），美国管理学家，任教于奥尔巴尼大学商学院，学术研究方向涉及领导力、权力与影响力、激励机制、培训与发展。

WAYS IN TO THE TEXT

- Born in 1947, John P. Kotter is an American management consultant* and scholar who currently teaches leadership* and management* at Harvard Business School and consults through his firm, Kotter International.

- *Leading Change* presents a comprehensive, eight-step model for how to carry out organizational change in large corporations.

- The book's use of practical examples and its wide applicability has made it one of the most influential books on organizational transformation ever written.

Who Is John P. Kotter?

John P. Kotter is an iconic figure in the field of organizational change and transformation, both as an academic and as a professional. He has written extensively on the topic and is widely read and acknowledged by managers and academics alike. He is often referred to as a "change and management guru."[1] In his writing, Kotter draws heavily on his practical experiences working with corporate organizations as a management consultant. The basis of his work throughout his career has been the translation of lessons he has learned about leadership and management from consulting and from study into recommendations that can be put into action. Managing transformation has been one of his major preoccupations for decades. In *Leading Change*, as in much of his work, Kotter opts for a conversational tone, using anecdote and analysis as if he were speaking directly to an audience of executives and business leaders.

Born in 1947, Kotter holds degrees from the Massachusetts Institute of Technology (MIT) and Harvard Business School, where he completed his PhD in 1972. He became a full professor at Harvard in 1980 at the age of 33, making him one of the youngest in the university's history. He continues to serve at Harvard as Konosuke Matsushita Professor of Leadership, Emeritus, teaching leadership and management. In addition to his academic work, Kotter is also chairman of Kotter International, a consulting firm he co-founded in 2008. The company has a broad client base, from large corporations such as Allstate, Genentech, and Microsoft, to governmental agencies such as the US Naval Air Systems Command and the Royal Canadian Navy.[2]

What Does *Leading Change* Say?

There are two core parts to *Leading Change,* which was first published in 1996. First, Kotter discusses what he sees as the eight most common mistakes companies make when trying to make changes. These are:

1. Tolerating complacency and failure to create a sense of urgency.
2. Failure to develop an effective coalition (an alliance of like-minded individuals).
3. Failure to construct a sensible vision.
4. Failure to communicate that vision.
5. Allowing obstacles, such as organizational structure and reluctant employees, to block the vision.

6. Failure to build on short-term successes.
7. Declaring victory too soon.
8. Not embedding successful changes in the corporate culture.*

Kotter notes that "none of these change errors would be that costly in a slower-moving and less competitive world."[3] However, in a rapidly changing economy, "making any of the eight errors common to transformation efforts can have serious consequences."[4] Changes that move too slowly can cause layoffs, budgetary squeezes, and have lasting effects on communities where the company exists.

To guide companies away from these errors, Kotter details an eight-step process for leading change that must be carried out in sequence:

1. Establish a sense of urgency.
2. Create the guiding coalition.*
3. Develop a vision and strategy.
4. Communicate the change vision.
5. Empower broad-based action.*
6. Generate short-term wins.*
7. Consolidate gains and produce more change.
8. Anchor new approaches in the culture.[5]

Another important feature of Kotter's change process is the distinction between management and leadership. He says "successful transformation is 70 to 90 percent leadership and only 10 to 30 percent management."[6] In a slower world, he argues, managerial talent was perhaps more important than leadership: "For most of this century, as we created thousands and thousands of large organizations for the first time in human history, we didn't have enough good managers to keep all those bureaucracies functioning."[7] By contrast, in an age of technological and industrial transformation, the "sacrifice, dedication, and creativity"[8] necessary for change must come from leaders rather than managers.

The core of *Leading Change* is Kotter's elaboration on the eight- step process and the practical examples he discusses to make the steps relatable. A typical example is his discussion of "Jerry," an "overworked division-level CFO (Chief Financial Officer) at a major oil company"[9] in the chapter on building a guiding coalition. Jerry is more "manager than leader" and is "naturally suspicious of calls for significant change." So it may initially seem not worth the effort to convert him to support a change process. He is likely to resist, and will probably not offer creative solutions.[10] If Jerry has some rank or status in the company, however, because of his seniority and experience, ignoring him or excluding him from a change effort will eventually backfire, so Kotter advises leaders to include "Jerry" in their planning. *Leading Change* is full of characters like Jerry, and to a large extent the success of the book is due to the relevance of these characters and their situations.

Why Does *Leading Change* Matter?

Leading Change is a valuable text for many different people.

Business students who know something of the problems associated with organizational transformation will be able to relate directly to the examples and concepts in the book. Such students may benefit from examining Kotter's examples as if they were genuine business cases: What is the market under analysis? Who are the characters involved? And how does Kotter explain the mistakes the characters make? Business students with ambitions towards leadership positions will learn the methods of one of the most influential change consultants of the last two decades. It is likely that students who fully absorb Kotter's approach will be able to interact more effectively with their own bosses when they enter the workplace.

The book is also of use to non-business students. Most of the principles in *Leading Change* apply equally well to any organizational setting. For example, Kotter advises change leaders trying to communicate their vision to "keep it simple" with "focused, jargon- free information" and to use "the power of metaphor, analogy, example, or just plain colorful language to communicate complicated ideas quickly and effectively."[11] He presents this advice in the context of a change effort in a large company, but it could equally well be applied to a start-up, a new marketing campaign, a congressional campaign, or a major research initiative in a university. Readers of all kinds who work in groups, regardless of their size or function, will find invaluable information in *Leading Change*.

Kotter instinctively values leadership over management. The "lifelong learner"* model Kotter presents at the end of the book is a challenge to continue to grow, both personally and professionally, throughout life. By using the concept of compounded growth* (growth that builds on itself) to describe personal development, Kotter suggests that significant transformations can result from small behavioral changes such as asking for critical feedback or taking risks.[12] *Leading Change* can serve as both business manual and self-help book.

1. "Kotter's 8-Step Change Model," Mind Tools, accessed May 21, 2015, http://www.mindtools.com/pages/article/newPPM_82.htm.

2. "Our Clients," Kotter International, accessed May 17, 2015, http://www.kotterinternational.com/clients/.

3. John P. Kotter, *Leading Change* (Boston: Harvard Business School Press, 1996), 15.

4. Kotter, *Leading Change*, 15.

5. Kotter, *Leading Change*, 20–2.

6. Kotter, *Leading Change*, 26.

7. Kotter, *Leading Change*, 27.

8. Kotter, *Leading Change*, 30.

9. Kotter, *Leading Change*, 60.

10. Kotter, *Leading Change*, 60.

11. Kotter, *Leading Change*, 91–2.

12. Kotter, *Leading Change*, 183.

SECTION 1
INFLUENCES

THE AUTHOR AND THE HISTORICAL CONTEXT

KEY POINTS

* *Leading Change* presents an eight-stage process to implement successful change in organizations.

* Kotter's experience as a management consultant* in many different industries makes his book both unique and practically useful.

* The book was first published in 1996 at a time of increasing globalization* and increasing uncertainty about how this would change ways of doing business.

Why Read This Text?

John P. Kotter wrote *Leading Change* in 1996, after his well-received article "Leading Change: Why Transformation Efforts Fail,"[1] published in the March-April 1995 issue of *Harvard Business Review*. The book, which has won many awards and is an international bestseller, is considered a landmark publication in the area of leadership* and change. Its central idea is to present an eight-stage process to implement change and aid transformation efforts in organizations, based on the author's personal experience of helping big businesses. The term "big" is important—Kotter's focus in *Leading Change* is transforming large firms, not small companies.

The book's practical tone and presentation is its key strength. Rather than focusing on academic arguments, Kotter presents his change principles clearly and succinctly, regularly using examples from real but mostly anonymous firms to support his ideas. The breadth of examples makes the book a useful guide for a wide audience. While not all readers will identify with each of the eight stages Kotter describes, it is likely that readers with experience in big firms will find at least some of his suggestions useful. *Leading Change* is also notable for its foresight. Kotter sets his argument about organizational change in the context of an increasingly global and fast-changing business environment. Today, his concerns about how to deal with rapid changes are even more appropriate.

> *"By any objective measure, the amount of significant, often traumatic change in organizations has grown tremendously over the past two decades. Although some people predict that most of the reengineering, restrategizing, mergers, downsizing, quality efforts, and cultural renewal projects will soon disappear, I think that is highly unlikely ... As a result, more and more organizations will be pushed to reduce costs, improve the quality of products and services, locate new opportunities for growth, and increase productivity."*
>
> —— John Kotter, *Leading Change*

Author's Life

John P. Kotter was born in 1947. He graduated from the Massachusetts Institute of Technology (MIT) in Electrical Engineering and Computer Science in 1968, then went on to do a Master of Science from MIT and later a Doctorate in Business Administration from Harvard Business

School. In 1972, Kotter joined the faculty of the Harvard Business School, where he was named full professor in 1980 at the age of 33. He continues to teach there today.

Over the course of his career, Kotter has written 18 books, including *Our Iceberg is Melting*, a *New York Times* bestseller published in 2006. In 2001, *Business Week* magazine named Kotter the premier leadership guru in the United States, based on a survey of 504 enterprises.[2] He is also the founder of Kotter International, which helps Global 5,000 companies*—a database of 5,000 corporations representing more than $50 trillion in revenue—implement change using the eight-step process introduced in this book.

According to Kotter, *Leading Change* draws exclusively on his own experiences as a business consultant with almost 100 companies over a period of 25 years. As he writes in the preface to the book: "This work is more personal than any I've previously published. I'm communicating here what I've seen, heard, and concluded on a set of interrelated topics that appear to be increasingly important."[3] Little is known publicly about the exact nature of Kotter's consulting work or the relationships he has with the companies in his examples. But he is internationally renowned in the area of leadership and change management. His position as a thought leader on organizational change gives credibility to his interpretations of these real-world cases.

Author's Background

Kotter's work has been influenced by globalization, which is characterized by rapid technological change,* international economic integration,* and the evolution of domestic markets* in more developed countries. The modern wave of globalization that began in the 1980s and forms the backdrop of *Leading Change* is tied to a number of events, including a series of free-trade* agreements that dismantled global trade barriers, reduced transport costs, and led to the willingness of companies to look abroad to lower production costs.

Kotter argues that because companies are not immune to global economic and social forces, they have had to embrace organizational change more intensely. Whereas businesses in the pre-globalized twentieth century may have been able to survive for several decades with very little internal transformation, Kotter suggests that is no longer the case now that markets are global. He writes: "Even companies that sell only in small geographic regions can feel the impact of globalization. The influence route is sometimes indirect: Toyota beats General Motors (GM), GM lays off employees, belt-tightening employees demand cheaper services from the corner dry cleaner."[4] This example highlights the potential unintended consequences of business decisions in a global marketplace. While Toyota was acting in its own interest only, its decisions had a direct impact on GM, which then had an indirect impact on many small businesses, including the dry cleaners that serviced GM employees.

---

1. John P. Kotter, "Leading Change: Why Transformation Efforts Fail," *Harvard Business Review* 73, no. 2 (1995): 59–67.

2. "Rating the Management Gurus," Bloomberg, October 14, 2001, accessed May 18, 2015, http://www.bloomberg.com/bw/stories/2001-10-14/rating- the-management-gurus.

3. John P. Kotter, *Leading Change* (Boston: Harvard Business School Press, 1996), x.

4. Kotter, *Leading Change*, 18.

MODULE 2
ACADEMIC CONTEXT

KEY POINTS

- The study of management* concerns the planning, structure, design, and effectiveness of institutions, particularly business organizations; by focusing on change efforts, *Leading Change* relates to many of these topics.
- Prior to Kotter's work, management studies* had shifted from focusing on objectives to studying relationships between employers and employees.
- Kotter based *Leading Change* on his own work, but was likely influenced by others developing similar change models at the same time.

The Work in its Context

John P. Kotter's *Leading Change* is an example of management studies, an area of business thought focused on understanding how organizations, specifically firms, plan and organize their resources to achieve their goals. A related, and in some cases overlapping, discipline is leadership studies,* which focuses on the role of leadership* in carrying out organizational objectives. Management and leadership studies can be loosely grouped into two categories: one is characterized by highly theoretical, sometimes mathematical studies of organizational behavior;* the other consists of practical guides intended for business leaders. *Leading Change* is an example of the second category.

Leading Change also fits into the more general area of

business and administration literature. Scholarly writing in this tradition can be both analytic and prescriptive, aimed at both academic and professional audiences. For example, an author may conduct an extensive research project, including surveys and statistical analysis, to determine how incentives in a firm influence performance. This kind of analysis would include observed results similar to those found in economics[*] and political science.[*] Another author may write a guidebook for managers during times of uncertainty using real-world examples and the author's own intuition. By its very nature, business literature is highly diverse, runs across numerous disciplines, and tends to overlap with areas of economics, sociology, mathematics, and history.

⌐ *"Management is doing things right. Leadership is doing the right things."*

——Peter Drucker, *Essential Drucker: Management, the Individual, and Society* ⌐

Overview of the Field

The modern academic study of management is often traced back to the work of Peter Drucker,[*] an Austrian American management consultant[*] and academic. Drucker's most notable contribution to the field was the Management by Objectives (MBO)[*] approach, which he described in his 1954 book, *The Practice of Management*. The MBO approach tasks managers with making decisions that lead the organization to specific results, taking into account changing external circumstances such as fluctuations in the economy and the behavior of other firms in the market. Drucker suggests that only by defining objectives beforehand can decisions be made effectively. He writes: "Objectives are needed in every area where performance and results directly and vitally affect the survival and prosperity of the business."[1] While managers may prefer to make decisions as simply and as free from judgment as possible—restricting the range of choices available so as to minimize errors—Drucker holds that applying judgment is one of the most important aspects of successful management.

Another scholar who contributed to the early development of management and leadership studies was Douglas McGregor,* whose book, *The Human Side of Enterprise*, published in 1960, introduced the Theory X and Theory Y* model of individual motivation.[2] In this context, "theory" refers to the assumptions managers make about their employees—in other words, managers tend to treat their employees in a certain way according to a preconceived theory about what motivates them. According to McGregor, Theory X employees are lazy and unmotivated, and so need close supervision, while Theory Y employees are ambitious and self-motivated. McGregor's work introduced managers to the idea that company performance can be affected by their own assumptions about employees' motivations. It also brought concepts from psychology and human behavior into management literature.

Academic Influences

During the 1990s, when Kotter developed the ideas for *Leading Change*, there was already a growing body of literature about so-called learning organizations* (valuing teamwork and collaborative models of management), organizational change, and transformation in general. For example, W. Warner Burke* and George Litwin* developed a model to understand the features common to successful change efforts.[3] Unlike Kotter's book, Burke and Litwin's paper explores the factors that *cause* change, not how managers can better bring about change. Similarly, Heather Haveman* wrote a paper in 1992 that argued against the position that change was harmful to an organization's performance. She suggested instead that "organizational change may benefit organizational performance and survival chances if it occurs in response to dramatic restructuring of environmental conditions and if it builds on established routines and competencies."[4] In other words: when circumstances require change, it will tend to be good for the company; when they do not, change may be harmful.

Some authors at the time, such as Peter Senge* and William Edwards Deming,* were also talking about quality control, teamwork, and adaptive organizations in the context of change efforts.[5] Senge and Deming both recognized the importance of globalization* and the challenges it represented. Indeed, one of Deming's suggestions to managers in a complex, global economy was to "eliminate management by objectives" and "substitute leadership."[6] Kotter was undoubtedly influenced by these writers and, while not responding directly to them in *Leading Change*, he incorporated some of their ideas into the book. It should be noted, however, that Kotter's work was predominantly based on his own experiences and intuition, not on the work of others.

1. Peter Drucker, *The Practice of Management* (New York: Harper Collins, 1954), 63.

2. Douglas McGregor, *The Human Side of Enterprise* (New York: McGraw-Hill, 1960).

3. W. Warner Burke and George H. Litwin, "A Causal Model of Organizational Performance and Change," *Journal of Management* 18, no. 3 (1992): 523–45.

4. Heather A. Haveman, "Between a Rock and a Hard Place: Organizational Change and Performance Under Conditions of Fundamental Environmental Transformation," *Administrative Science Quarterly* 37, no. 1 (1992): 48.

5. Peter M. Senge, *The Fifth Discipline: The Art and Practice of the Learning Organization* (London: Century Business, 1991); and William Edwards Deming, *Out of the Crisis* (Cambridge, MA: MIT Press, 2000).

6. Deming, *Out of the Crisis*, 24.

MODULE 3
THE PROBLEM

KEY POINTS

* Academics in the 1990s were concerned with the content, context, and process of organizational change.

* Other models of change proposed at the time are similar to those in *Leading Change*, but they emphasize different aspects of the change process.

* Kotter may well have been aware of the work of others operating in the same area, but he makes no direct reference to it.

Core Question

When John P. Kotter published *Leading Change* in the 1990s, organizational change was an active area of debate, largely due to the rapidly changing business environment resulting from globalization.* Authors at the time were writing about organizational change based around three themes: [1]

- Content: attempting to define common factors in both successful and unsuccessful change efforts (see, for example, W. Warner Burke* and George Litwin's* model and Thomas Vollman).*[2]

- Context: examining forces and conditions in the internal and external environment of organizations to see how they affect the change process (see, for example, Nils Finstad* and Heather Haveman).*[3]

- Process: focusing on the actual actions undertaken while initiating change at the level of external environment, firm, and individual (see, for example, Kurt Lewin,* Timothy Galpin,* Achilles A.Armenakis*).[4] Particular emphasis was placed on how to *improve* change processes, rather than just *understand* them.

Kotter's work in *Leading Change* relates to the third theme. He defines different stages in the process of implementing change in organizations, with a series of actions that can be taken at the individual and firm level. Kotter was asking a core question: what factors hold back change efforts in large organizations, and what steps can be taken to improve organizations' ability to implement these efforts? It is important to understand the meaning of "change" in this context. By "change," Kotter means "restructuring, re-engineering, re-strategizing, acquisitions, downsizing, quality programs, and cultural renewal."[5] In other words, he is referring to any modification to the function or structure of the business. Kotter was not unique in asking this question. The originality of his argument lies in the broad sweep of his analysis and his ability to make it relevant to both academics and business people.

> *"It has been said that arguing against globalization is like arguing against the laws of gravity."*
> —— *The Globalist,* "Kofi Annan on Global Futures"

The Participants

Two scholars, whose work in the 1990s most resembles Kotter's, are Arnold Judson* and Timothy Galpin. Judson developed a model for implementing change that consists of five phases:

1. Analyze and plan the change.
2. Communicate the change.
3. Gain acceptance for new behaviors.
4. Change from the status quo to the desired state.
5. Consolidate the new state.[6]

A key element of Judson's model was to offer reward programs and incentives to minimize resistance from reluctant managers. Such ideas are absent from Kotter's model.

Galpin offered another model to guide implementation of the change process.[7] Rather than a series of key stages, he imagined a wheel made of nine wedges. The wedges of the model were:

1. Establish the need to change.
2. Develop and share a vision of that change.
3. Analyze the current situation.
4. Generate recommendations.
5. Detail the recommendations.
6. Pilot-test the recommendations.
7. Prepare the recommendations for rollout.
8. Roll out recommendations.
9. Measure, reinforce, and refine change.

Galpin's model is similar to Kotter's. Indeed, there are similarities between all three models; but while all end with building the change effort into the corporate culture,* there are clear differences in emphasis.

The Contemporary Debate

Although Kotter may have been aware of other authors writing on organizational change in the 1990s, *Leading Change*, like the *Harvard Business School* article it is based on, makes no direct reference to the work of others in the field. In fact, Kotter constructs his argument exclusively from his own experiences and intuition—there are no references provided. Unlike his predecessors, Kotter developed a comprehensive account of the entire change process from start to finish.

Rather than referring to other scholarly works, Kotter introduces *Leading Change* as an extension of the ideas he presented in his previous publications, including *A Force for Change: How Leadership Differs from Management*, and *Corporate Culture and Performance*.[8] As he writes in the preface: "Unlike my previous books, *Leading Change* is not filled with footnotes or endnotes. I have neither drawn examples or major ideas from any published source except my own writing nor tried to cite evidence from other sources to bolster my conclusions."[9] It is possible that this decision set *Leading Change* apart from other similar books of the period.

---

1. Achilles A. Armenakis and Arthur G. Bedeian, "Organizational Change: A Review of Theory and Research in the 1990s," *Journal of Management* 25 (1999): 293–315.

2. See W. Warner Burke and George H. Litwin, "A Causal Model of Organizational Performance and Change," *Journal of Management* 18, no. 3 (1992): 523–45; and Thomas E. Vollmann, *The Transformation Imperative: Achieving Market Dominance Through Radical Change* (Boston: Harvard Business School Press, 1996).

3. Nils Finstad, "The Rhetoric of Organizational Change," *Human Relations* 51, no. 6 (1998): 717–40; and Heather A. Haveman, "Between a Rock and a Hard Place: Organizational Change and Performance Under Conditions of Fundamental Environmental Transformation," *Administrative Science Quarterly* 37, no. 1 (1992): 48–75.

4. Kurt Lewin, "Frontiers in Group Dynamics II: Channels of Group Life; Social Planning and Action Research," *Human Relations* 1 (1947): 143–53; Timothy J. Galpin, *The Human Side of Change: A Practical Guide to Organization Redesign* (San Francisco: Jossey-Bass Publishers, 1996); and Achilles A. Armenakis, Stanley G. Harris, and Hubert S. Feild, "Paradigms in Organizational Change: Change Agent and Change Target Perspectives," *Public Administration and Public Policy* 87 (2001): 631–58.

5. John P. Kotter, *Leading Change* (Boston: Harvard Business School Press, 1996), ix.

6. Arnold S. Judson, *Changing Behavior in Organizations: Minimizing Resistance to Change* (Cambridge, MA: Blackwell, 1991).

7. Galpin, *The Human Side of Change*.

8. John P. Kotter, *A Force for Change: How Leadership Differs from Management* (New York: Free Press, 1990); and John P. Kotter and James L. Heskett, *Corporate Culture and Performance* (New York: Free Press, 1992).

9. Kotter, *Leading Change*, x.

MODULE 4
THE AUTHOR'S CONTRIBUTION

KEY POINTS

* *Leading Change* is an expansion of a *Harvard Business Review* article that appeared in 1995, in which John Kotter laid out an eight-stage process for carrying out change in organizations.

* Kotter follows a simple formula in the book, first introducing a step to change, then illustrating it with an example, and elaborating on it through discussion.

* *Leading Change* largely builds on Kotter's previous work, though existing works on change from writers such as Chris Argyris* and Douglas McGregor* operate in similar areas.

Author's Aims

John P. Kotter's main aim in writing *Leading Change* was to expand on the ideas he presented in his 1995 *Harvard Business Review* article "Leading Change: Why Transformation Efforts Fail."[1] The article was well received, jumping to first place among reprints sold. The response Kotter had from readers inspired him to write more about the topic: "First, managers read the list of mistakes organizations often make when trying to effect real change and said *Yes! This is why we have achieved less than we hoped.* Second, readers found the eight-stage framework compelling."[2] In order to expand on the article, Kotter included "dozens and dozens of examples of what seems to work and what doesn't."[3] These additions not only made the book more interesting, but also clarified the vision behind Kotter's ideas and made his argument more credible.

In the full-length book, Kotter was able to do what he had envisaged, and the road map to change appears both feasible and practical.The book appeals primarily to senior managers, as it prepares them for the process of change, which can often be daunting without experience or guidance. Employees may find the book less relevant to their own experience, as the steps Kotter describes unfold in a top-down manner. Indeed, most of the responsibility for implementing change in Kotter's model is given to leaders in the organization, not to those lower in the corporate structure. The book's continued popularity, however, demonstrates that it remains core reading for managers and that the examples included were both appropriate and realistic.

> "In the summer of 1994, I wrote an article for the Harvard Business Review *entitled 'Leading Change: Why Transformation Efforts Fail.' It was based on my analysis of dozens of initiatives over the prior 15 years to produce significant useful change in organizations ... Even as I was finishing that piece I knew I wanted to write more on the subject, so I began this book shortly thereafter."*
>
> ——John Kotter, *Leading Change*

Approach

Apart from the introductory and closing sections, *Leading Change* follows a simple formula: introduce one of the steps to change, and elaborate on that step with examples and general discussion. The book consists of relatively simple ideas presented in a straightforward manner. Kotter uses examples that will endear managers to his way of thinking. In fact, the purpose of many of the examples seems to be to give readers a reference point. Consider this example of meetings at a global pharmaceuticals company suffering from lagging sales: "Visit a typical management* meeting at the company and you begin to wonder if all the facts you gathered about the firm's revenues, income, stock price, customer complaints, competitive situation, and morale could have been wrong ... The pace is often leisurely. The issues being discussed can be of marginal importance."[4] Most of Kotter's readers will have had involvement with complacent organizations. His aim with this example is clearly to build trust with the readers, and connect his ideas to their own experience.

Contribution in Context

Leading Change follows the same framework that was introduced in Kotter's original article, but with a more detailed discussion and numerous examples. Kotter had written many books on organizational change and leadership* before *Leading Change*, and his key ideas can be traced back to his earlier works, including *A Force for Change: How Leadership Differs from Management* and *Corporate Culture and Performance*. These two works, and his later book *The New Rules*,[5] contain similar ideas to *Leading Change* and are still in print. To some extent the best reference point for how Kotter's ideas have evolved is his own previous writing on change and transformation.

Earlier works on change management focused on aspects such

as managers' actions or behavior, not with change as a step-by-step process. Two notable examples are Chris Argyris's books on how senior managers behave in difficult situations and Douglas McGregor's *The Human Side of Enterprise*, which identifies factors and forces that can create a positive environment for employees' performance.[6] These writers form a background to Kotter's work, but *Leading Change* itself largely exists outside the academic tradition on change.

---

1. John P. Kotter, "Leading Change: Why Transformation Efforts Fail," *Harvard Business Review* 73, no. 2 (1995): 59–67.

2. John P. Kotter, *Leading Change* (Boston: Harvard Business School Press, 1996), ix.

3. Kotter, *Leading Change*, ix.

4. Kotter, *Leading Change*, 37.

5. John P. Kotter, *A Force for Change: How Leadership Differs from Management* (New York: Free Press, 1990); John P. Kotter and James L. Heskett, *Corporate Culture and Performance* (New York: Free Press, 1992); John P. Kotter, *The New Rules: Eight Business Breakthroughs to Career Success in the 21st Century* (New York: Free Press, 1997).

6. Chris Argyris, *Interpersonal Competence and Organizational Effectiveness* (Homewood, IL: Dorsey Press, 1962); Chris Argyris, *Organization and Innovation* (Homewood, IL: R. D. Irwin, 1965); and Douglas McGregor and Joel Cutcher-Gershenfeld, *The Human Side of Enterprise* (New York: McGraw- Hill, 2006).

SECTION 2
IDEAS

MAIN IDEAS

KEY POINTS

- John Kotter's *Leading Change* focuses on how business organizations can evolve and the rise of globalization.*
- Kotter lists eight common mistakes organizations make when attempting change and offers an eight-step change process.
- Kotter presents his ideas simply, with minimal jargon, and with reference to several examples.

Key Themes

John P. Kotter's *Leading Change* revolves around the theme of how business organizations can evolve and transform. The word "change" appears throughout the book, and has many meanings. As examples of change, Kotter imagines a business being forced to "reduce costs, improve the quality of products and services, locate new opportunities for growth, and increase productivity"— though this list is likely incomplete.[1] Kotter associates change with any introduction of new business practices in response to changes in the external business environment. Importantly, his steps for implementing change apply to whatever change or challenge faces the business, whether it's an accounting shift or a new manufacturing procedure. The steps should apply equally well to a pharmaceutical company, an oil company, or a large university.

A second theme, which is closely related to the first, is the necessity of change due to globalization—the transformation of trade regulations* and transport costs that have led to markets reaching well beyond their physical boundaries. For Kotter, globalization is the reason for many of the change initiatives described in the book.As he writes: "A globalized economy is creating more opportunities for everyone, forcing firms to make dramatic improvements not only to compete and prosper but also to merely survive."[2] In other words, whereas before globalization change was desirable, in a global economy it is *vital* for survival.

> "To some degree, the downside of change is inevitable. Whenever human communities are forced to adjust to shifting conditions, pain is ever present. But a significant amount of the waste and anguish we've witnessed in the past decade is avoidable."
>
> —— John Kotter, *Leading Change*

Exploring the Ideas

Leading Change addresses the key theme of organizational change by developing a roadmap for managers to follow as they implement change in their organizations. The text has two main components: a list of common errors and mistakes made by managers, and an eight-stage change process.

Based on Kotter's analysis of change initiatives in the corporate world, he identifies eight common errors that managers make while implementing change. These are as follows:

1. Changing organizations without creating a sense of urgency among the employees—in other words, "allowing too much

complacency."[3] If employees do not feel a need to change their own behavior, they will not understand the seriousness of the situation or help the change process.

2. Managers failing to create a guiding coalition* with key members of the organization. While change efforts may survive for a while without a powerful coalition, "sooner or later, countervailing forces undermine the initiatives."[4]

3. Lack of a sensible vision.

4. Miscommunication, under-communication, or lack of communication.

5. Failing to create an enabling environment. Organizations sometimes fail to change because of obstacles such as a rigid "organizational structure," including "supervisors who refuse to adapt to new circumstances."[5]

6. Failing to create short-term wins,* such as "money-saving course corrections" (or small reforms) or partial implementation of new production methods that help build momentum for the larger change effort.[6]

7. Declaring victory before the change process is complete.

8. New behaviors not being rooted deeply enough in the corporate culture,* so that changes are not anchored properly for continued success.[7]

Kotter's solution to these problems is his sequential eight-stage process. A manager may go through multiple stages at the same time, but Kotter warns that skipping any of the steps, or not giving them sufficient attention, will hurt the change process, which will not "build and develop in a natural way."[8] The process is as follows:

1. Establish a sense of urgency.
2. Create the guiding coalition.
3. Develop a vision and strategy.
4. Communicate the change vision.
5. Empower broad-based action.
6. Generate short-term wins.
7. Consolidate gains and produce more change.
8. Anchor new approaches in the corporate culture.[9]

Each of the steps is discussed in detail in *Leading Change*, with a separate chapter dedicated to each, featuring advice on implementation supported by examples from different companies. For example, in step 3, vision refers to "a picture of the future with some implicit or explicit commentary on why people should strive to create that future."[10] One of the examples Kotter uses to show the importance of vision is a "medium-size retail business." An executive of this company introduced a promising plan that was challenged for being "too fuzzy and soft."[11] In spite of this opposition, the executive was able to successfully implement his vision by relying on the first two steps in the change process: building coalitions and establishing a sense of urgency.

Language and Expression

Kotter expresses his ideas in a very simple, non-academic, and comprehensible style using practical examples. The placement and content of these examples are crucial for understanding his ideas. For example, in a chapter about complacency, Kotter introduces a case study of a "major global pharmaceuticals company" that "has had more than its share of challenges over the past few years."[12] Citing conversations with employees, Kotter observes that the employees are aware of a problem, but: "The energy level is rarely high."[13] Well-placed examples like this, based on real-life situations, make the author's propositions more convincing and easier to relate to.

Leading Change is mostly free of business and economic jargon. Even readers with only a limited experience of management* or corporate culture should easily understand each of the eight change strategies. When Kotter uses business language such as "short term wins,"* "corporate culture," or "new vision," he presents the ideas in a way that does not require specific knowledge. This makes his text accessible to a very wide audience.

---

1. John P. Kotter, *Leading Change* (Boston: Harvard Business School Press, 1996), 3.

2. Kotter, *Leading Change*, 18.

3. Kotter, *Leading Change*, 4.

4. Kotter, *Leading Change*, 6.

5. Kotter, *Leading Change*, 10.

6. Kotter, *Leading Change*, 12.

7. Kotter, *Leading Change*, 4–15.

8. Kotter, *Leading Change*, 24.

9. Kotter, *Leading Change*, 20–2.

10. Kotter, *Leading Change*, 68.

11. Kotter, *Leading Change*, 80.

12. Kotter, *Leading Change*, 36.

13. Kotter, *Leading Change*, 36.

MODULE 6
SECONDARY IDEAS

KEY POINTS

• John Kotter's secondary ideas include: the differences between leadership* and management;* characteristics of the organization of the future; and characteristics of lifelong learners.*

• Kotter emphasizes the importance of urgency and a lack of complacency in organizations of the future.

• Kotter's discussion of globalization* as a coming force is less important today as it is now already a fact of business life.

Other Ideas

An important secondary idea in John P. Kotter's *Leading Change* is the role and importance of leadership in carrying out change. Kotter differentiates between management and leadership, and believes managers must adopt the characteristics of leaders to change and transform their firms successfully. He associates management with stagnant bureaucracies and effective leadership with transformative organizations:* "With a strong emphasis on management but not leadership, bureaucracy and an inward focus take over. But with continued success, the result mostly of market dominance, the problem often goes unaddressed and an unhealthy arrogance begins to evolve. All these characteristics then make any transformation effort much more difficult."[1]

Kotter does not dismiss management skills entirely, and argues that effective management is required for the important tasks of planning, budgeting, organizing, staffing, and problem solving. In contrast, leadership is the process that helps organizations form and then adapt to significant changes in the environment. According to Kotter: "Successful transformation is 70 to 90 percent leadership and only 10 to 30 percent management."[2]

Two related ideas concern the characteristics of the "organization of the future" and how to develop the traits of successful leaders in a globalized economy.[3] Kotter argues that as rapid change becomes more important in the business environment, organizations must be able to maintain the following: a strong sense of urgency, effective teamwork among executives, good communication of vision, the empowerment of a broad base of employees, and an ability to change the company culture. Further, Kotter discusses the ideal executive of the future. Perhaps most importantly, he says that future leaders must be dedicated to "lifelong learning."

> "Major transformations are often associated with one highly visible individual ... This is a very dangerous belief."
> —— John Kotter, *Leading Change*

Exploring the Ideas

Referring to his argument that leadership is more valuable than management, Kotter argues that the problem is not so much about managing change, but that managers do not have sufficient leadership qualities. Managers in the traditional sense create an "overmanaged and underled" corporate culture of bureaucracy, arrogance, and insularity.[4] Rather than removing management altogether, Kotter suggests finding and developing managers who have leadership qualities.

In the final chapters of the book, Kotter looks to the future. In a chapter entitled "The Organization of the Future," he describes what he believes will be the keys to managerial success in the future, assuming the rate of change in the business environment continues. One of the most important characteristics of these organizations, Kotter says, is maintaining a sense of urgency. He writes: "A higher rate of urgency does not imply ever present panic, anxiety, or fear. It means a state in which complacency is virtually absent, in which people are always looking for both problems and opportunities, and in which the norm is 'do it now.'"[5] This urgency is closely related to another of Kotter's predictions: broad-based empowerment.* Citing several technology companies that have successfully created a culture of empowerment, Kotter says that in organizations that deal with a high level of change, you will find "unusually flat hierarchies, little bureaucracy, a propensity for risk-taking, workforces that largely manage themselves, and senior-level people who focus on providing leadership."[6] In other words, in successful organizations of the future, meddling management will be replaced by empowered employees and executives focused on leadership.

In order to ensure that organizations can find suitable employees for these roles, Kotter describes his ideal future leader: the lifelong learner. According to Kotter, lifelong learners are defined by five characteristics: a willingness to take risks, honest self-assessment, aggressive collection of the opinions of others, careful listening, and openness to new ideas.[7] He argues it is more important to continue to learn over time than to excel at any given point in life.[8]

Overlooked

The core ideas of *Leading Change* are easy to digest and therefore little has been overlooked. Naturally, the eight-stage process has been the most widely cited feature of the book, and less attention has been given to Kotter's secondary ideas. In the two chapters where Kotter looks beyond the eight-stage process to the future of organizations and leaders, he is careful to manage expectations. "Speculating on the future is always hazardous," he notes, "but the discussion presented in this book has rather clear implications."[9] The areas where Kotter is less sure of his arguments have been less widely circulated and shared by readers. However, the list-like nature of Kotter's main argument has made that argument easy to share as a standalone entity separate from the book itself.

It is true that Kotter's discussion of globalization in *Leading Change* has declined in importance.When he wrote the book in the 1990s, the prospect of widespread global markets was relatively new; in the twenty-first century it is commonplace. It is therefore unlikely that an executive today would use Kotter's book to highlight the many challenges created by global markets. Globalization is now a given, not an emerging phenomenon requiring special thought or preparation.

1. John P. Kotter, *Leading Change* (Boston: Harvard Business School Press, 1996), 27.
2. Kotter, *Leading Change*, 26.
3. Kotter, *Leading Change*, 161.
4. Kotter, *Leading Change*, 43.
5. Kotter, *Leading Change*, 162.
6. Kotter, *Leading Change*, 167.
7. Kotter, *Leading Change*, 183.
8. Kotter, *Leading Change*, 181.
9. Kotter, *Leading Change*, 162.

ACHIEVEMENT

KEY POINTS

* In *Leading Change*, John Kotter was successful in expanding on his ideas about how change in business could happen most effectively.
* The book has proved to be useful in areas outside of business, including war studies and health service research.
* *Leading Change* would benefit from a broader cultural and geographic perspective. The book's focus is purely American.

Assessing the Argument

John P. Kotter's intention with *Leading Change* was to expand on the ideas presented in his earlier article of the same name, and in this he was successful. Though there were other change models in the 1990s, Kotter's is unique in focusing specifically on the *process* of change and in his practical style of presentation. While others were more overtly academic in their discussion of change, Kotter maintained a close eye on the business world. The examples he uses make his model compelling.

Despite this success, Kotter's change model is not universal. His work is based solely on examples from the Western world. Organizations in the developing world and fragile states face far more turbulent and volatile environments. They are more vulnerable to natural disasters and to uncertainty in their political and technological environment. The context, environment, and macroeconomic* environment that create change will be different and may require a different framework for change management.

Another important contextual factor at the time the text was written was the North American Free Trade Agreement (NAFTA),* established in 1994, which opened free trade* between the United States, Canada, and Mexico. This meant increased competition and greater challenges for firms, which had to change and transform their business processes so they did not lose market share. It is likely that NAFTA contributed to the popularity of *Leading Change*, as managers had to plan for a more integrated world economy.

> "Comparing today's business environment to 20 years ago, it strikes me that wins—and an intentional approach to producing them—have only increased in importance as the fuel of large-scale sustainable change.The energy they produce can overpower the effects of speed, distraction, and dilution that conspire against change efforts.They can help break down change-blocking silos. So, too, the complexity of globalization, which increasingly feels like a high-speed game of 3-D chess."
>
> ——Gregg LeStage, "How Have Kotter's Eight Steps for Change Changed?"

Achievement in Context

Leading Change has not only gained acclaim and recognition in the field of business and management,* but has also been used by academics and practitioners in other social science disciplines. Its eight-stage model provides a road map for managers of all kinds and has been used in war studies, health services research, information and technology (IT) management, industrial relations, and much more. Case studies have been designed around the model to teach students about leading change efforts. The work's academic application has proved extremely useful for researchers and scholars. Studies in health services research have used Kotter's framework to reform the state-level health services in the United Kingdom. IT management specialists have used it to explain the introduction of new technology in organizations and to minimize resistance among workers confronting new structures, processes, and machinery.

Although *Leading Change* is based on examples from the private sector and corporate world, the model has been widely used to explain change and public service reform across various social sectors such as health services and education. Its universal appeal is also evident in its academic application across various fields in the social sciences. This wide application of Kotter's work may have surprised him, as the book was initially intended primarily for senior management and practitioners in the corporate sector.

Leading Change has also been important in management development workshops. Such workshops are now featured as a development opportunity in every organization. Kotter's model is sequential, has clear stages, and is targeted at senior management: it serves as an excellent tool to analyze complex situations.

Limitations

Kotter describes a general process of change, which should be applicable to almost all change situations. One of the biggest limitations of the book, however, is its lack of examples from the developing world. The author has mainly used examples from his own observations, derived from his experience with organizations in North America, and he focuses on a sample of firms that are mainly from one country: the United States. The eight-stage framework can still be applied universally, and the steps and propositions are reasonably generic. Nevertheless, managers are advised to keep both the internal and external environment in mind while making an organizational analysis.

Context is another limitation. Organizational change and transformation is no longer a "one-time" activity as it may have been in the mid-1990s. It is now more of a permanent feature, as firms continuously change and transform to maintain their competitive edge. The importance of context, especially geographical context, cannot be ignored, but Kotter does not focus on national differences. Change is also no longer only an American or North American phenomenon; as business becomes global, organizations must predict and respond to change around the world and manage it in tandem. A comparative analysis including evidence from other parts of the world would greatly improve Kotter's original analysis.

PLACE IN THE AUTHOR'S WORK

KEY POINTS

* John P. Kotter's career has been consistently concerned with the analysis and implementation of change efforts in organizations; he has carried out these efforts both as a scholar and as a management consultant.*
* Kotter defines his own career in two stages, the first stage was based around research, the second around implementation.
* *Leading Change* is one of Kotter's most important books, but he had already built a significant reputation before its publication in 1996.

Positioning

John P. Kotter wrote *Leading Change* after already writing several books and articles on change and leadership.* In his 1979 article, "Choosing Strategies for Change," co-authored with Leonard Schlesinger,* Kotter introduced many of the ideas that would later appear in *Leading Change*. He and Schlesinger highlight the importance of recognizing "people's limited tolerance for change"[1] as a key resistance factor. This observation is closely related to the sense of urgency Kotter describes in *Leading Change*. In *A Force for Change: How Leadership Differs from Management*, published in 1990, Kotter is mostly concerned with the role of effective leadership in change efforts. The distinction between leadership and management,* a key feature of *Leading Change*, appears throughout that book too: "Leadership and management differ in terms of their primary function. The first can produce useful change, the second can produce orderly results which keep something working efficiently."[2]

The most direct forerunner to *Leading Change*, however, was Kotter's 1995 article "Leading Change: Why Transformation Efforts Fail."[3] This article provided the first instance of Kotter's eight steps for carrying out change. Since the publication of *Leading Change*, Kotter has refined his ideas in several books and articles, most notably *Our Iceberg is Melting*, published in 2006. That book tells the story of a group of penguins stranded on a melting iceberg and the importance of creating a sense of urgency to save themselves.Again this is a theme that is prominent in *Leading Change* and earlier Kotter works.

> "Up until this project, all of my past work, research now spanning many decades, has used the same formula. Find cases representing the highest 10% or 20% of performers. Observe what they do. Talk to people who have lived in those situations. Then do the same for the average performers and the laggards. Look for patterns that show the differences. Report those factors with an emphasis on factors that you can change—to take average performance to high or lagging results at least up to the norm."
>
> —— John P. Kotter, *Accelerate: Building Strategic Agility for a Faster-Moving World*

Integration

Kotter divides his career into two phases: a research phase, which took place from 1972 to 2008, and an implementation phase from

2008 onward.[4] The research phase is dominated by the development of the eight-stage process for carrying out change that is detailed in *Leading Change*. Kotter's work has almost exclusively focused on how organizations behave in times of transformation. As such, his work has covered topics including leadership, management, risk taking, and organizational behavior.* The theme of managing change is ever present in his writing, if sometimes only on a background level.

The implementation phase of Kotter's career is mostly defined by his work at Kotter International, the consulting firm he co-founded in 2008. Kotter International's mission statement is closely tied to the themes of Kotter's research, specifically *Leading Change*. The eight-stage process features prominently on the Kotter International website. For instance, there is a blog post on the website written by Gregg LeStage,* entitled "Is your organization developing change managers or change leaders?" In the blog, LeStage emphasizes the distinction between management and leadership: "The difference between a change manager and a change leader—as noted in the definitions above—is significant. Change managers typically drive incremental change, ensuring work is done on time and within budget. Change leaders, on the other hand, are less adverse to getting 'messy' and taking risks, influencing and inspiring behaviors that lead to large-scale transformation."[5] The similarity between the tone and content of the Kotter International website and *Leading Change* suggests a high degree of integration of Kotter's work throughout his career.

Significance

Leading Change is among Kotter's most influential works. The Kotter International website emphasizes the book's importance: "For 40 years, Harvard Business School Professor John Kotter has engaged in broad and deep studies investigating why 70% of businesses fail to execute their strategies and only 5% meet or exceed them ... Chief among [Kotter's] successes was the development of the award-winning 8-Step Process for Leading Change in 1996."[6] *Leading Change* is also one of Kotter's best-selling books, and was selected in 2011 as one of the 25 most influential management books by *Time Magazine*.[7]

Leading Change remains one of Kotter's major works, but it would be an overstatement to say Kotter built his reputation on the book. Prior to its publication, he was already a well-recognized figure in business scholarship and had held a prominent position at Harvard Business School for more than two decades. Also, *Leading Change* is by no means Kotter's most academic or rigorous book; it includes no footnotes or references to other writers. The book is best viewed as a distillation of Kotter's thinking up to the mid-1990s and one of the foundations on which he built his subsequent work.

---

1. John Kotter and Leonard Schlesinger, "Choosing Strategies for Change," *Harvard Business Review* (2008 reprint), accessed May 21, 2015, https://hbr.org/2008/07/choosing-strategies-for-change/ar/1.

2. John P. Kotter, *A Force for Change: How Leadership Differs from Management* (New York: Free Press, 1990), 7.

3. John P. Kotter, "Leading Change: Why Transformation Efforts Fail," *Harvard Business Review* 73, no. 2 (1995): 59–67.

4. "About Us," Kotter International, accessed May 21, 2015, http://www.kotterinternational.com/about-us/.

5. Gregg LeStage, "Is your organization developing change managers or change leaders?" accessed May 21, 2015, http://www.kotterinternational. com/insights/organization-developing-change-managers-change-leaders/.

6. Kotter International, "About Us."

7. "The 25 Most Influential Business Management Books," *Time Magazine*, August 9, 2011, accessed May 21, 2015, http://content.time.com/time/ specials/packages/article/0,28804,2086680_2086683_2087679,00. html.

SECTION 3
IMPACT

THE FIRST RESPONSES

KEY POINTS

* *Leading Change* has been criticized for being too rigid and for placing too much emphasis on top-down leadership.*
* While Kotter has had minimal interaction with his critics, he made a significant modification to the model in 2012 to account for a more flexible business environment.
* Critics of *Leading Change* have noted that a changing business world has required alterations to Kotter's model.

Criticism

One of the criticisms of John P. Kotter's work in *Leading Change* is that, given the complexity of the change process, no one model can be entirely effective. Kotter's book has been immensely popular: so if his model is correct, the success rate of change efforts in large organizations should have increased; but this does not seem to have been the case. As Carolyn Aiken and Scott Keller write: "Kotter's research revealed that only 30 percent of change programs succeed. Since the book's release, literally thousands of books and journal articles have been published on the topic, and courses dedicated to managing change are now part of many major MBA* (Master of Business Administration) programs. Yet in 2008, a McKinsey* survey of 3,199 executives around the world found, as Kotter did, that only one transformation in three succeeds. Other studies over the past 10 years reveal remarkably similar results. It seems that, despite prolific output, the field of change management hasn't led to more successful change programs."[1]

With this in mind, Aiken and Keller suggest that the practice of change management is "in need of a transformation through an improved understanding of how humans interpret their environment and choose to act."[2] In other words, rigid models such as Kotter's may only be of limited effect.

Another criticism of the book concerns Kotter's description of change as a top-down practice. In his 2009 article "Rebuilding Companies as Communities," Henry Mintzberg* concedes that "Kotter's approach sounds sensible enough and has probably worked," but challenges the focus on a "driving leader" to bring about change. He writes: "Perhaps it's time to rebuild companies not from the top down or even the bottom up but from the middle out—through groups of middle managers who bond together and drive key changes in their organization."[3] Although Kotter mentioned the need to create short-term wins* for employees, top-down change can lead to frustration among employees. Further, the sequential, step-by-step nature of Kotter's model does not take into account the many unexpected problems that might have to be dealt with for a change effort to succeed.

Some writers have challenged Kotter's views on management* and leadership. Gary Yukl,* a management theorist, has argued that leadership is part of the managerial tasks that every manager must undertake in an organization and that leadership and management skills are equally important to run and transform organizations successfully.[4]

> *"Even though it is difficult to identify any consensus regarding a framework for organizational change management, there seems to be an agreement on two important issues. Firstly, it is agreed that the pace of change has never been greater than in the current business environment ... Secondly, there is a consensus that change, being triggered by internal or external factors, comes in all shapes, forms, and sizes."*
>
> ——Rune Todnem By, *Organizational Change Management: A Critical Review*

Responses

Kotter has had little public interaction with his critics, though he has since revised his eight-step *Leading Change* model. In his article, "Accelerate!" published in the *Harvard Business Review* in 2012,[5] Kotter replaced the model with a "strategy system" that "expands on the eight-step method I first documented 15 years ago."[6] There are three main differences between the eight-step model and the strategic model. First, the step model was "often used in rigid, finite, and sequential ways," whereas the strategy model recognizes factors that accelerate change, which are "concurrent and always at work."[7] This modification may have been inspired by changing circumstances in the business environment—as the rate of change has increased, maintaining a linear, step-by-step progression has become impossible. Second, the step process was led by a "small, powerful group," while "accelerators pull in as many people as possible from throughout the organization to form a 'volunteer army.'"[8] Finally, the accelerator framework is built around a view of the organization that is informed by social networks, rather than as a top-down structure.

While Kotter does not cite critics of his work as inspirations for these changes, he references three scholars whose work led him in this direction: Michael Porter,* a professor at Harvard Business School, who provided Kotter with the "wake-up call that organizations need to pay attention to strategy much more explicitly and frequently;"[9] Clayton Christensen,* also of Harvard, whose work showed him how poorly organizations manage technological change* in a fast-paced environment; and Daniel Kahneman,* who referred to "the brain as two coordinated systems, one more emotional and one more rational."[10] It is notable that none of these scholars focus on organizational change in particular.

Conflict and Consensus

As the business environment is complex and constantly changing, no single model of transformation and change can be definitive. Some trends in the literature being produced on the subject, however, as well as Kotter's own alterations to his model, suggest a degree of consensus. Part of that consensus is that change models must incorporate new methods, such as social network analysis:* this can give a more accurate picture of how information is transmitted through an organization than the official company structure might suggest. Such tools were only partially developed in 1996, so it is not surprising that Kotter's original book did not make use of them. Another part of this general consensus is that organizational change is unlikely to unfold as a sequence of events and instead is constantly evolving and chaotic. As Leandro Herrero* writes in a 2014 review of

Leading Change: "The linear, sequential world has gone."[11] Herrero intended this as a critique of Kotter's model, but Kotter himself had already disowned the sequential nature of his model.

Another aspect of consensus around the themes in *Leading Change* is that transformation is an integral part of today's business environment, and that organizations should dedicate resources to understanding how they can most effectively transform.When Kotter wrote the book in 1996, he had to spend considerable time convincing his audience that managing globalization* would require more focused attention on change efforts. This is no longer required, as globalization has been fully integrated into the business environment.

---

1. Carolyn Aiken and Scott Keller, "The Irrational Side of Change Management," April 2009, accessed May 21, 2015, http://www.mckinsey. com/insights/organization/the_irrational_side_of_change_management.

2. Aiken and Keller, "The Irrational Side of Change Management."

3. Henry Mintzberg, "Rebuilding Companies as Communities," *Harvard Business Review*, July 2009, accessed May 21, 2015, https://hbr.org/2009/07/rebuilding-companies-as-communities.

4. Gary A. Yukl, *Leadership in Organizations* (Upper Saddle River, NJ: Prentice Hall, 2010).

5. John P. Kotter, "Accelerate!" *Harvard Business Review*, November 2012, accessed May 21, 2015, https://hbr.org/2012/11/accelerate.

6. Kotter, "Accelerate!"

7. Kotter, "Accelerate!"

8. Kotter, "Accelerate!"

9. Kotter, "Accelerate!"

10. Kotter, "Accelerate!"

11. Leandro Herrero, "John Kotter's 8 Step Change Management model is the best change model of the last Century. Why this is still alive in 2014 is beyond me," October 21, 2014, accessed May 21, 2015, http://leandroherrero.com/john-kotters-8-step-change-management-model-is-the-best-change-model-of-the-last-century-why-this-is-still-alive-in-2014-is-beyond-me/.

MODULE 10
THE EVOLVING DEBATE

KEY POINTS

* *Leading Change* was one of the first models of the process of organizational change, and inspired later work in the field.
* Change research is categorized in three ways: by the rate of occurrence, by how it comes about, and by scale. *Leading Change* is in the second category.
* *Leading Change* has been highly influential and helped inspire other models from scholars such as Peter Senge,* Jeffrey Liker,* and James Franz,* whose work examines change processes in a wider set of circumstances.

Uses and Problems

When John P. Kotter's *Leading Change* was first published in 1996, many authors already saw change as an inevitable part of the business environment. As time passed, it was recognized that change should be a permanent feature of all organizational strategies, and more people started developing their own change process models. This ever-growing literature emphasized the importance of change and how it could be approached, but gave little observed data to prove the theories and models that were presented.

Leading Change was written at a time when organizations were approaching business transformation in terms of reengineering,* total quality management,* reorganization, and technological change.* The popularity of Kotter's article had already shown that people were thinking about organizational change, but were unclear how to approach it to get the best results. The publication of the book marked the beginning of *process* models of organizational change: Kotter made the process less mysterious and less unpredictable. He showed that the results of change could be foreseen and that his model, if followed correctly and in sequence, could lead to successful organizational transformation.

Later works by authors such as Peter Senge, Jeffrey K. Liker, and James K. Franz developed Kotter's ideas so they could be applied to a wider range of circumstances. Their work focused on the theme of organizational change under chaotic and complex conditions. They took into consideration contingency factors* (unknown influences or events) and environments (both internal and external) that force organizations to change and adapt. Because such forces cannot be planned for, the change effort cannot be described in a step-by-step, sequential manner: the authors therefore propose the idea of *cyclical** change.

> *"Just as organizations are going to be forced to learn, change, and constantly reinvent themselves in the twenty-first century, so will increasing numbers of individuals. [Kotter] goes on to say that as the rate of change increases, the willingness and ability to keep developing, that is to keep learning, become central to career success for individuals and to economic success for organizations."*
>
> —— Gary Tomlinson, "Book Review on 'Leading Change' by John Kotter"

Schools of Thought

Change literature can be categorized into three main streams or schools of thought:[1]

- Change characterized by the *rate* of occurrence.
- Change characterized by *how* it comes about.
- Change characterized by *scale*.

Kotter's work belongs to the second school, where change is dealt with by how it comes about. This school traces its roots to Kurt M. Lewin's* work.According to Lewin, a successful change initiative will pass through three stages: unfreezing the current stage; change, or moving to the new level; and refreezing the level.[2] This model proposes a planned approach to change and argues that we need to discard old behavior, structures, processes, and culture. Other notable authors who have worked on the planned approach and have developed similar models are Richard Luecke* and Bernard Burnes.* Burnes criticized the idea that there is one change strategy that is best, arguing that each model merely seeks to replace one set of prescriptions with another. He believed instead that organizations do have real choices in what they change and how they change it.[3]

The authors in this school of thought have mostly put forward planned, sequential models of change that are similar to Kotter's. Some have taken environmental factors into consideration and adapted their work to include contingency factors: things do not always go according to the plan and at times it becomes impossible to stick to the plan. Managers need to be cautious, deal with contingencies, and tailor their plans accordingly. Kotter's model of change serves as a benchmark for all subsequent models of change in this school of thought. Later developments in the field have proven that his model is a good starting point for managing change and transformation in organizations.

In Current Scholarship

Today, the topic of organizational change is an active area of debate and scholarship, though attention has moved from understanding the *process* of change as a sequence of steps to understanding change more broadly. Many of the major thinkers in this area have now moved on from Kotter's work as they apply new research systems to the change process. Kotter's ideas are probably best represented in the work of members of his own consulting firm, Kotter International. The firm publishes regular articles on change in a similar framework and tone to *Leading Change*. A recent piece, for example, written by Gregg LeStage,* asks, "Is your organization developing change managers or change leaders?" The article asks readers to choose between a set of options, such as: "We keep all projects on budget" or "We're actively mobilizing resources" to determine whether their organization is producing change leaders or change managers.[4] This distinction first appeared in *Leading Change* and continues to be an important part of Kotter's framework.

Another article discusses the question of whether or not leadership* can be taught, noting: "As Professor John Kotter has so often written, the most effective leaders know how and when to appeal to peoples' heads and hearts: it's all about balance. This is never so important as when change is the order of the day or year—or era."[5] Yet another piece discusses the decision of President Obama* to use the Internet show "Between Two Ferns" to advertise the changes to health care introduced by his Affordable Care Act* of 2010. The author connects the event to the techniques of successful communicators—an important theme in *Leading Change*—by concluding that "superior communicators must willingly deliver outside of their comfort zones."[6]

1. Rune Todnem By, "Organizational Change Management: A Critical Review," *Journal of Change Management* 5 (2005): 369–80.

2. Kurt Lewin, "Frontiers in Group Dynamics II: Channels of Group Life; Social Planning and Action Research," *Human Relations* 1 (1947): 143–53.

3. Richard Luecke, *Managing Change and Transition* (Boston: Harvard Business School Press, 2003); and Bernard Burnes, "No Such Thing as ... a 'One Best Way' to Manage Organizational Change," *Management Decision* 34, no. 10 (1996): 11–18.

4. Gregg LeStage, "Is your organization developing change managers or change leaders?" accessed May 21, 2015, http://www.kotterinternational. com/insights/organization-developing-change-managers-change-leaders/.

5. Gregg LeStage, "Can Leadership be Taught," accessed May 21, 2015, http://www.kotterinternational. com/insights/can-leadership-be-taught/.

6. Shaun Spearmon, "Why 'Between Two Ferns' Is Obama's Health Care Secret Weapon," accessed May 21, 2015, http://www.kotterinternational. com/insights/two-ferns-obamas-health-care-secret-weapon/.

IMPACT AND INFLUENCE TODAY

KEY POINTS

* *Leading Change* is a seminal book in change management literature and continues to have an influence today.

* A debate continues regarding the differences and relative benefits and drawbacks of linear versus more complex change models.

* Some critics of Kotter's position challenge the rigidity of his model, suggesting that common sense and flexibility are more important than prescribed steps.

Position

John P. Kotter's *Leading Change* is a classic in the field of change management and continues to have an influence today. Much of the influence of the book, however, is channeled through Kotter's subsequent work, which has refined and revised aspects of his eight-step model for change.

There is no single formula for organizational transformation, but following a plan such as Kotter's eight-stage framework can increase the chances of successful organizational transformation. In his book on leadership* theory, Peter Northouse* acknowledges the importance of leadership in bringing about change,and suggests that management* and leadership are not only complementary, but integral to successful managers.[1] *Leading Change*'s value has been enhanced by such later works.

Change and transformation have affected all organizations for the last two to three decades. The concept of organizational change and transformation in the 1990s was not very different from what it is today. But change and transformation in organizations has become more complex. Despite more than two decades of research in organizational change and transformation, change still tends to be "reactive, discontinuous and ad hoc with a reported failure rate of around 70 percent of all change programs initiated."[2] The current debate still revolves around finding a suitable framework for organizational change management. Despite many authors coming up with change frameworks, the above figure shows that more work needs to be done. Kotter's book continues to play an important role in such research.

> "Virtually all organizations on earth go through a very similar life cycle.They begin with a network-like structure, sort of like a solar system with a sun, planets, moons and even satellites. Founders are at the center. Others are at various nodes working on different initiatives. Action is opportunity seeking and risk taking, all guided by a vision that people buy into ... Over time, a successful organization evolves through a series of stages ... into an enterprise that is structured as a hierarchy and is driven by well-known managerial processes."
>
> —— John Kotter, *Accelerate: Building Strategic Agility for a Faster-Moving World*

Interaction

Leading Change does not directly conflict with contemporary thinkers or schools of thought, but it does bring together the author's earlier ideas and works on the importance of leadership and change as a process. The last 20 years have seen a great deal of research around this theme, and there continue to be differences between linear change models and complex change models. Linear models suggest a step-by-step process—if managers in a company carry out each step in order, the initiative should be successful. In contrast, complex change models describe change as an ongoing and nonlinear process.

Despite this research and a number of articles and books on change management, most change initiatives still do not achieve their desired results.[3] This presents a challenge to theorists proposing change models—particularly models that have been put into practice such as Kotter's. The time is ripe to revisit the models and come up with new theories of change and transformation. Malcolm Higgs* and Deborah Rowland's* 2005 article[4] reports that in practice, change approaches based on complexity (for example the approaches of Peter Senge,* and Jeffrey K. Liker* and James K. Franz)*[5] rather than linearity (for example those of Kotter himself, and of Michael Hammer* and James Champy)*[6] have proven more successful.

The Continuing Debate

Change literature is a diverse area of research and debate. Kotter has modified his change model to adapt to current business conditions and now incorporates a more flexible approach based on recent research in the behavioral sciences. Some writers still challenge Kotter's model in its original form. The consultant Leandro Herrero* has criticized Kotter for continuing to promote his rigid, step-by-step change model, even though the complexity of the world has shown that greater flexibility is needed. He writes: "No revolution will ever be made with Kotter steps. Not the 1996, not the 2014 steps. Yet, maybe 'revolution' is not the target of industrial reinvention, so, no problems here. But, dare to ignore it. For great management, read Kotter, say thanks, and then look outside the window."[7]

Notably, this most recent criticism is of Kotter's 2014 rewrite of his change model, not the 1996 version presented in *Leading Change*. Herrero suggests Kotter's new, less linear model is still too rigid. As he says, mockingly referring to Kotter's own suggestion that managers carry out the steps "concurrently and continuously": "Welcome to 2014, or 2015. The 'run the steps concurrently and continuously' has taken around 19 years to materialize as a piece of advice, as his website says, 'after extensive research'. This non-accelerated discovery can only be matched by Vatican speed."[8] Criticisms such as this are rare, but express an alternative view that may be less visible due to the popularity and prestige of Kotter's work.

---

1. Peter Guy Northouse, *Leadership: Theory and Practice* (Thousand Oaks, CA: Sage Publications, 2004).

2. Rune Todnem By, "Organisational Change Management: A Critical Review," *Journal of Change Management* 5 (2005): 378.

3. Malcolm Higgs and Deborah Rowland, "All Changes Great and Small: Exploring Approaches to Change and Its Leadership," *Journal of Change Management* 5, no. 2 (2005): 121–51; and John P. Kotter, *A Force for Change: How Leadership Differs from Management* (New York: Free Press, 1990).

4. Higgs and Rowland, "All Changes Great and Small."

5. Peter M. Senge, *The Fifth Discipline: The Art and Practice of the Learning Organization* (London: Century Business, 1991); and Jeffrey K. Liker and James K. Franz, *The Toyota Way to Continuous Improvement : Linking Strategy and Operational Excellence to Achieve Superior Performance* (New York: McGraw-Hill, 2011).

6. John P. Kotter, *Leading Change* (Boston: Harvard Business School Press, 1996); and Michael Hammer and James Champy, *Reengineering the Corporation: A Manifesto for Business Revolution* (New York: HarperBusiness, 1993).

7. Leandro Herrero, "Change management: Harvard, you have a problem," accessed May 21, 2015, http://leandroherrero.com/change-management- harvard-you-have-a-problem/.

8. Herrero, "Change management: Harvard, you have a problem."

MODULE 12
WHERE NEXT?

KEY POINTS

* *Leading Change* will continue to be an important book in change literature, but its importance will lessen as new methods add to our understanding of organizational change.*

* Scholars such as Julie Battilana* of Harvard Business School and others will move Kotter's ideas forward by expanding the range of study techniques and focusing on employees rather than executives.

* *Leading Change* was written at a time when change was an emerging topic and its clarity, comprehensiveness, and use of practical examples has made it a seminal work.

Potential

John P. Kotter's *Leading Change* remains a milestone in the field of organizational change. Understanding and carrying out change is seen as much more important today than it was in 1996. Businesses face new challenges every day and have to keep in touch with the latest market trends and technologies. This forces them to transform their methods, culture, and processes to keep up with global forces and competition. As long as adaptation remains a crucial aspect of business life, the principles in *Leading Change* will continue to be relevant.

The future potential of *Leading Change* is tied to the development of change models that reflect the flexible organizations of the future. Kotter predicted the emergence of flexible businesses, but business structures have transformed even more rapidly than even he imagined. One criticism of *Leading Change* has been that the model centers on the senior ranks of management* in an organization. As Kayleigh O'Keefe writes: "The 8-step model puts enormous pressure on leaders and managers, but doesn't ask for much of employees. Managers are expected to ease fears, have all the answers, be expert communicators, and manage talent. Employees are expected to follow along."[1] Kotter's eight-stage model could be improved by integrating feedback from employees closer to the implementation of changes. A greater focus on uncertainty, and on employee participation in change efforts could also improve Kotter's model.

> *"Formal authority is, of course, an important source of influence. Previous research has shown how difficult it is for people at the bottom of a typical organization chart—complete with multiple functional groups, hierarchical levels, and prescribed reporting lines—to drive change. But most scholars and practitioners now also recognize the importance of the informal influence that can come from organizational networks."*
>
> ——Julie Battilana and Tiziana Casciaro, "The Network Effects of Great Change Agents"

Future Directions

One scholar who may move the study of change leadership* in this direction is Julie Battilana, associate professor at Harvard Business School. Battilana's work has used network analysis—the use of graph theory and network models to study social behavior—to understand how great change leaders operate in a business. In "The Network Secrets of Great Change Agents," Battilana and her co-author Tiziana Casciaro used a social network model to study 68 change initiatives in the National Health Service* in the United Kingdom. The model looks at individuals in the organization and how they are connected, allowing the authors to determine whether or not an individual is enabling change, resisting it, or is indifferent.

Their network analysis uncovered three aspects of change leadership Kotter's model does not include. First, "Change agents who were central in the organization's informal network had a clear advantage, regardless of their position in the formal hierarchy."[2] In other words, individuals who are well connected in a company can be crucial for change even if they do not have formal power. Second, individuals who "bridged disconnected groups," (groups that otherwise would not be connected) were better at implementing major changes, while individuals with "cohesive networks" (networks in which most or all of the individuals are connected) were better at bringing about minor changes. Finally, maintaining associations with "fence-sitters," or individuals "ambivalent about a change," was beneficial for carrying out change efforts. In contrast, maintaining associations with resistors could reduce the probability that a change effort will be successful. This research begins to fulfill the potential aim of *Leading Change*—to understand at the level of the individual how change efforts flow through an organization. Network analysis can replace Kotter's discussion of leading coalitions with a more rigorous investigation of how coalitions work and what kinds of personalities form them.

Summary

Since its publication, *Leading Change* has had considerable influence in both the classroom and the boardroom. It is one of the dominant perspectives on how organizations think about change efforts in large organizations. The combination of Kotter's practical eight-step model and his numerous examples make the book a useful guide for potential leaders at any level. For two decades, the book has had a powerful influence on how managers think about organizational transformation; knowledge of *Leading Change* should enable students to interact more effectively with their managers on entering the workforce.

Leading Change was written at a time when organizations were just beginning to recognize the importance of change in their organizations. Since then, change has become an ever-present feature of the business environment. Kotter presents his work in a very simple, approachable, and comprehensible way. The book identifies common mistakes that managers make that hinder change: when managers read the book, they can relate to the mistakes and find similarities with their own experience. This conversational tone is *Leading Change's* defining feature and ensures that readers at all levels will find the book not only useful, but also enjoyable.

---

1. Kayleigh O'Keefe, "Where Kotter's 8 Steps Gets it Wrong," *CEB Blogs*, accessed May 21, 2015, https://www.executiveboard.com/blogs/where-kotters-8-steps-gets-it-wrong/.

2. Julie Battilana and Tiziana Casciaro, "The Network Secrets of Great Change Agents," *Harvard Business Review*, accessed May 21, 2015, https://hbr. org/2013/07/the-network-secrets-of-great-change-agents/ar/1.

GLOSSARY OF TERMS

1. **Affordable Care Act (known as Obamacare):** a United States statute passed in 2010 that represents the most significant reform of the American health care system since 1965.The act requires Americans to hold some kind of health insurance and established insurance exchanges to create competition in the insurance market.

2. **Broad-based empowerment:** representation and participation in decision-making among a large group of employees.

3. **Compounded growth:** a concept describing growth that is exponential or logarithmic, i.e. growth that builds on itself.The principle of compounded growth implies both personal and professional development.

4. **Contingency factors:** aspects of the business environment that influence planning and strategy, including changes in the external environment and technology.

5. **Corporate culture:** the shared values, beliefs, and behaviors of a company's employees and management.A company's corporate culture will determine how people interact within the company and how it handles its business transactions and external relationships.

6. **Cyclical change:** an approach to change leadership that emphasizes that change cannot be understood on a step-by-step basis, and offers leaders alternative guidelines for leading change.

7. **Domestic market:** the market for goods and services in a given country.

8. **Economics:** social science that studies the production, distribution, and consumption of both goods and services.

9. **Free trade:** a policy of not restricting trade between countries, usually by removing tariffs and other trade barriers.

10. **Global 5,000 companies:** a database of 5,000 companies, both private and public, representing several industries and more than $50 trillion in revenue.

11. **Globalization:** the process by which the world seems to become increasingly smaller.This is often the result of advances in communication and growing interactions of culture, commerce, religion, and politics among groups that

normally would not have been in contact with one another.

12. **Guiding coalition:** a group of people with the ability and drive to lead a change effort in an organization.

13. **International economic integration:** this can refer to agreements such as GATT (General Agreement on Tariffs and Trade). GATT was a multilateral agreement between nations to regulate international trade. The purpose was to reduce tariffs and other trade barriers for mutual benefits among countries. GATT was signed in 1947 and lasted until 1994, when it was replaced by the World Trade Organization (WTO).

14. **Leadership:** this typically refers to a quality or set of qualities, including vision, charisma, persistence, power, and intelligence, that translate into the carrying out of effective social change. Leadership can also be the process of carrying out change by enlisting the support of others.

15. **Leadership studies:** a multidisciplinary academic discipline with the goal of identifying the characteristics of successful leadership and understanding the context of leadership in organizations.

16. **Learning organization:** a term coined by Peter Senge and his colleagues at the MIT Sloan School of Management and used in his book *The Fifth Discipline:The Art and Practice of the Learning Organization. The Fifth Discipline* talks about an organization that has five features: systems thinking, personal mastery, mental models, shared vision, and team learning. Learning organizations value teamwork and collaborative models of management.

17. **Lifelong learning:** the process of continually growing both personally and professionally.

18. **Macroeconomics:** the branch of economics that deals with large-scale economic factors, such as economic growth, the money supply, and long-term trends in technology.

19. **Management:** the function in businesses and organizations that coordinates the efforts of different branches of the company. Managers are typically tasked with achieving objectives in such a way that minimizes costs or effort.

20. **Management by Objectives (MBO):** an approach to management developed by Peter Drucker in which results are tied to objectives in the firm, which are, in turn, tied to managerial behavior.

21. **Management consulting:** the process of helping firms with their performance, typically by analyzing processes and strategy in the company.

22. **Management studies:** an academic discipline dedicated to understanding the internal processes of business organizations and how those processes can be changed to maximize business objectives.

23. **MBA:** short for Master of Business Administration, this is a master's degree, originally awarded in the United States in the late nineteenth century as a measure of academic excellence when industrialization started to happen.

24. **McKinsey:** refers to McKinsey & Company, a multinational management consulting firm, which produces analysis to help companies make good management decisions.

25. **National Health Service (NHS):** the publicly funded health care system of the United Kingdom.

26. **North American Free Trade Agreement (NAFTA):** a free trade agreement that went into effect in January 1994 between Mexico, Canada, and the United States. The goal of the agreement was to eliminate trade barriers between the three countries.

27. **Organizational behavior:** the study of individual and group activity in an organization.

28. **Political science:** social science that studies political institutions and processes.

29. **Reengineering:** using information technology to re-invent the way a company does its business—improving productivity and cutting costs.

30. **Short-term wins:** successes that are likely to be a step towards a larger goal rather than the ultimate goal.

31. **Social network analysis:** the use of network models and graphs to study social structures and the ways in which social structures operate in other institutions.

32. **Technological change:** this refers to faster and better communication (the Internet revolution), better means of transportation, and information networks that connect people globally.

33. **Theory X and Theory Y model:** a model of organizational behavior developed by Douglas McGregor in which managers operate using a theory—Theory X or Theory Y—to understand their employees. Under Theory X, employees are assumed to be inherently lazy, while under Theory Y they are self-motivated.

34. **Total Quality Management:** a management principle where every member of a company must commit to maintaining the highest standards possible in every area to improve customer satisfaction.

35. **Trade regulation:** a field of law covering the analysis and regulation of international trade. Particular concern is given to limiting anti-competitive practices such as unfair pricing or monopoly.

36. **Transformative organizations:** an organization that changes the way it operates in a significant way. Transformation can refer to the production process, the hiring process, or any major feature of the organization.

PEOPLE MENTIONED IN THE TEXT

1. **Chris Argyris (1923–2013)** was an American business scholar who studied the relationship between organizational structures and firm behavior. He is also associated with the development of action science, or the study of how human beings design their actions in the face of challenges.

2. **Achilles A. Armenakis** is an American business scholar who currently teaches at Auburn University. His primary research interest is change management.

3. **Julie Battilana** is a French business scholar who currently teaches at Harvard Business School. Her work focuses on how individuals and organizations can move away from deeply seated norms in order to change their behavior.

4. **W. Warner Burke** is an American professor of psychology and education at Teachers College at Columbia University. He maintains a workgroup studying the Burke-Litwin model of organizational change at Columbia.

5. **Bernard Burnes (b. 1953)** is a professor of organizational change at the Stirling Management School. His research covers the way in which different approaches to change promote or undermine ethical behavior in organizations.

6. **James Champy (b. 1942)** is a management consultant and authority on organizational change and business reengineering and renewal.

7. **Clayton Christensen (b. 1952)** is a professor at Harvard Business School and is regarded as one of the top experts on innovation and growth. His ideas have been widely used in organizations around the world.

8. **William Edwards Deming (1900–93)** was an American engineer and management consultant. He had a wide-ranging career, but one of his scholarly contributions is the Total Quality Management Movement, which is considered to have been born with his book *Out of Crisis*. In that book, Deming describes what managers should do to create lasting organizational change.

9. **Peter Drucker (1909–2005)** was an Austrian American management consultant and scholar who is considered the father of modern management. He helped develop the practical foundations of the modern business entity, and is known for his Management by Objectives (MBO) approach.

10. **Nils Finstad** is a Norwegian scholar of organizational change who has taught at

Bodø Regional University.

11. **James K. Franz** is an American businessman who serves as vice president of global operations at Toyota Way Academy.

12. **Timothy Galpin** is an American management professor at Colorado State University. He also serves as a business consultant on topics ranging from strategic planning, restructuring, and organizational change.

13. **Michael Hammer (1948–2008)** was an American author and engineer whose Business Process Reengineering (BPR) approach to management has been highly influential.

14. **Heather Haveman** is an American professor of organizational theory at the University of California, Berkeley. Her work investigates how organizations, and the people in them, evolve in the face of external and internal changes.

15. **Leandro Herrero** is a consultant, clinical psychologist, and lecturer who serves as CEO of the Chalfont Project, which oversees the Viral Change initiative, dedicated to the creation and implementation of large-scale behavioral and cultural change.

16. **Malcolm Higgs** is professor of human resource management and organization behavior at Southampton Business School. His academic interests include change management, particularly the link between positive emotions and change leadership.

17. **Arnold S. Judson** is a writer and management consultant who has written on change efforts and served as president of the Judson Company Inc., a strategic management consultancy based in Boston.

18. **Daniel Kahneman (b. 1934)** is an Israeli American psychologist, professor emeritus at Woodrow Wilson School at Princeton University, and Nobel Memorial Prize Winner in Economic Sciences.

19. **Gregg LeStage (b. 1965)** is Executive Vice President of Kotter International where he is responsible for global business development as well as working directly with clients.

20. **Kurt M. Lewin (1890–1947)** was a German American psychologist, known

for his pioneering work in the field of social and organizational psychology. He also provided a framework for looking at the factors (forces) that influence social situations, called Force Field Analysis. Force Field Analysis has been used in studies on organizational change to identify the relevant forces that affect the process of change.

21. **Jeffrey K. Liker** is an American professor of industrial and operations engineering at the University of Michigan, and owner of Liker Lean Advisors, a consulting firm. His work has studied the success of management techniques such as those used at Toyota.

22. **George Litwin** is an American organizational psychologist who has taught at Harvard Business School and whose work studies the characteristics of successful leaders.

23. **Richard Luecke (b. 1943)** is the author of a number of books on business and management including *Entrepreneur's Toolkit* (2004) and *The Busy Manager's Guide to Delegation* (2009).

24. **Douglas McGregor (1906–64)** was a management scholar who spent much of his career at the Massachusetts Institute of Technology. Perhaps McGregor's most important contribution was to introduce human behavior into the analysis of organizations.

25. **Henry Mintzberg (b. 1939)** is a Canadian scholar and consultant who has written several books, including *Managers not MBAs* and *Simply Managing*. His work focuses on managerial work, strategy formation, and forms of organizing.

26. **Peter Northouse** is a professor emeritus of communication in the School of Communication at Western Michigan University. His work focuses on models of leadership, leadership assessment, and group dynamics.

27. **Barack Obama (b. 1961)** is the 44th president of the United States. He is notable for being the first African American president and for introducing the first major health insurance reform act in decades, the Patient Protection and Affordable Care Act of 2010.

28. **Michael Porter (b. 1947)** is a professor at Harvard Business School, known for

his five forces model.

29. **Deborah Rowland** is founder of Lead Free Consultancy, a firm that provides change management advice to corporations. She is also the co-author of *Sustaining Change: Leadership That Works*, a guidebook for implementing change.

30. **Leonard Schlesinger** is a professor at Harvard Business School whose work studies the role of effective leaders in organizations.

31. **Peter Senge (b. 1947)** is an American systems scientist who currently teaches at the Massachusetts Institute of Technology. He is best known for his book *The Fifth Discipline*, which developed the theory of the learning organization.

32. **Thomas Vollmann (1937–2009)** was an American business professor who was considered a leading figure in the area of manufacturing control systems.

33. **Gary Yukl (b. 1940)** is an American management scholar who teaches at the University of Albany School of Business. His academic interests include leadership, power and influence, motivation, training, and development.

WORKS CITED

1. Argyris, Chris. *Interpersonal Competence and Organizational Effectiveness.* Homewood, IL: Dorsey Press, 1962.

2. *Organization and Innovation.* Homewood, IL: R. D. Irwin, 1965.

3. Armenakis, Achilles A., and Arthur G. Bedeian. "Organizational Change: A Review of Theory and Research in the 1990s." *Journal of Management* 25 (1999): 293–315.

4. Armenakis, Achilles A., Stanley G. Harris, and Hubert S. Feild. "Paradigms in Organizational Change: Change Agent and Change Target Perspectives." *Public Administration and Public Policy* 87 (2001): 631–58.

5. Barnett, William P., and Glenn R. Carroll. "Modeling Internal Organizational Change." *Annual Review of Sociology* 21 (1995): 217–36.

6. Burke, W. Warner, and George H. Litwin. "A Causal Model of Organizational Performance and Change." *Journal of Management* 18, no. 3 (1992): 523–45.

7. Burnes, Bernard. "No Such Thing as ... a 'One Best Way' to Manage Organizational Change." *Management Decision* 34, no. 10 (1996): 11–18.

8. By, Rune Todnem. "Organisational Change Management: A Critical Review." *Journal of Change Management* 5 (2005): 369–80.

9. Conner, Daryl. *Leading at the Edge of Chaos: How to Create the Nimble Organization.* New York: John Wiley, 1998.

10. Deming, William Edwards. *Out of the Crisis.* Cambridge, MA: MIT Press, 2000.

11. Finstad, Nils. "The Rhetoric of Organizational Change." *Human Relations* 51, no. 6 (1998): 717–40.

12. Galpin, Timothy J. *The Human Side of Change: A Practical Guide to Organization Redesign.* San Francisco: Jossey-Bass Publishers, 1996.

13. Hammer, Michael, and James Champy. *Reengineering the Corporation: A Manifesto for Business Revolution.* New York: HarperBusiness, 1993.

14. Haveman, Heather A. "Between a Rock and a Hard Place: Organizational Change and Performance Under Conditions of Fundamental Environmental Transformation." *Administrative Science Quarterly* 37, no. 1 (1992): 48–75.

15. Higgs, Malcolm, and Deborah Rowland. "All Changes Great and Small: Exploring Approaches to Change and Its Leadership." *Journal of Change Management* 5, no. 2 (2005): 121–51.

16. Judson, Arnold S. *Changing Behavior in Organizations: Minimizing Resistance to Change*. Cambridge, MA: Blackwell, 1991.

17. Kotter, John P. *A Force for Change: How Leadership Differs from Management*. New York: Free Press, 1990.

18. "Leading Change: Why Transformation Efforts Fail." *Harvard Business Review* 73, no. 2 (1995): 59–67. Reprinted in *HBR's 10 Must Reads: On Change Management* (Boston: Harvard Business School Press, 2011).

19. *Leading Change*. Boston: Harvard Business School Press, 1996.

20. "Leading Change: A Conversation with John P. Kotter." *Strategy & Leadership* 25 (1997): 18–23.

21. *The New Rules: Eight Business Breakthroughs to Career Success in the 21st century*. New York: Free Press, 1997.

22. "Accelerate!" *Harvard Business Review* 90, 11 (2012): 43–58.

23. Kotter, John P., and James L. Heskett. *Corporate Culture and Performance*. New York: Free Press, 1992.

24. Kotter, John P., and Holger Rathgeber. *Our Iceberg Is Melting: Changing and Succeeding Under Any Conditions*. New York: St Martin's Press, 2006.

25. LeStage, Gregg, "How Have Kotter's Eight Steps for Change Changed." *Forbes*, March 5, 2015. Accessed June 17, 2015. http://www.forbes.com/sites/johnkotter/2015/03/05/how-have-kotters-eight-steps-for-change-changed/.

26. Lewin, Kurt. "Frontiers in Group Dynamics II: Channels of Group Life; Social Planning and Action Research." *Human Relations* 1 (1947): 143–53.

27. Liker, Jeffrey K., and James K. Franz. *The Toyota Way to Continuous Improvement : Linking Strategy and Operational Excellence to Achieve Superior Performance*. New York: McGraw-Hill, 2011.

28. Luecke, Richard. *Managing Change and Transition*. Boston: Harvard Business

School Press, 2003.

29. Lunenburg, Fred C. "Leadership Versus Management: A Key Distinction— At Least in Theory." *International Journal of Management, Business and Administration* 14, no. 1 (2011): 1–4.

30. McGregor, Douglas, and Joel Cutcher-Gershenfeld. *The Human Side of Enterprise*. New York: McGraw-Hill, 2006.

31. Mintzberg, Henry. "Rebuilding Companies as Communities." *Harvard Business Review* 87, nos. 7/8 (2009): 140–3.

32. *Moran, John W., and Baird K. Brightman. "Leading Organizational Change." Career Development International* 6, no. 2 (2001): 111.

33. Northouse, Peter Guy. *Leadership: Theory and Practice*. Thousand Oaks, CA: Sage Publications, 2004.

34. Pettigrew, A. M., R. W. Woodman, and K. S. Cameron. "Studying Organizational Change and Development: Challenges for Future Research." *Academy of Management Journal* 44, no. 4 (2001): 697–713.

35. Porter, Michael. "How Competitive Forces Shape Strategy." *Harvard Business Review* 57, no. 2 (1979): 137–45.

36. Senge, Peter M. *The Fifth Discipline: The Art and Practice of the Learning Organization*. London: Century Business, 1991.

37. *The Dance of Change: The Challenges of Sustaining Momentum in Learning Organizations*. New York: Currency/Doubleday, 1999.

38. Vollmann, Thomas E. *The Transformation Imperative: Achieving Market Dominance Through Radical Change*. Boston: Harvard Business School Press, 1996.

39. Yukl, Gary A. *Leadership in Organizations*. Upper Saddle River, NJ: Prentice Hall, 2010.

40. Zaleznik, Abraham. "Managers and Leaders: Are They Different?" *Harvard Business Review* 55, no. 5 (1977): 67–78.

原书作者简介

约翰·P.科特是一位备受尊敬的学者和企业顾问，多年来一直为美国大公司提供变革咨询服务。科特生于 1947 年，毕业于麻省理工学院（理学学士、理学硕士）和哈佛大学（商务管理博士），现为哈佛商学院领导力教授。他的公司，科特国际，为微软等大型企业及美国政府部门提供咨询服务。科特的作品以务实著称，善用鲜活实例，向各类致力变革的组织提供咨询服务。

本书作者简介

雅米娜·萨尔曼博士毕业于爱丁堡大学组织管理博士专业，现任职于巴基斯坦旁遮普大学管理科学院。

尼克·布罗顿毕业于加利福尼亚理工学院和伦敦政治经济学院，目前在帕蒂兰德研究生院从事研究工作，是一名助理政策分析师。他当下的研究方向涉及临终关怀分配方法设计、缩小劳动力市场技能缺口及风投冒险行为的偏见分析。

世界名著中的批判性思维

《世界思想宝库钥匙丛书》致力于深入浅出地阐释全世界著名思想家的观点，不论是谁、在何处都能了解到，从而推进批判性思维发展。

《世界思想宝库钥匙丛书》与世界顶尖大学的一流学者合作，为一系列学科中最有影响的著作推出新的分析文本，介绍其观点和影响。在这一不断扩展的系列中，每种选入的著作都代表了历经时间考验的思想典范。通过为这些著作提供必要背景、揭示原作者的学术渊源以及说明这些著作所产生的影响，本系列图书希望让读者以新视角看待这些划时代的经典之作。读者应学会思考、运用并挑战这些著作中的观点，而不是简单接受它们。

ABOUT THE AUTHOR OF THE ORIGINAL WORK

John P. Kotter is a highly respected academic and business consultant with many years of practical experience advising major US corporations on change. Born in 1947, he has degrees from Massachusetts Institute of Technology and Harvard University, and is currently professor of leadership at Harvard. His company, Kotter International, consults for large corporations such as Microsoft, and for US government agencies. Kotter's work is characterized by its down-to-earth tone, using practical examples to advise those in all walks of organizational life who must grapple with change.

ABOUT THE AUTHORS OF THE ANALYSIS

Dr Yaamina Salman holds a PhD in organisational management from the University of Edinburgh. She is currently teaching at the Institute of Administrative Sciences at the University of the Punjab in Pakistan.

Nick Broten was educated at the California Institute of Technology and the London School of Economics. He is doing postgraduate work at the Pardee RAND Graduate School, and works as an assistant policy analyst at RAND. His current policy interests include designing distribution methods for end-of-life care, closing labour market skill gaps, and understanding biases in risk-taking by venture capitalists.

ABOUT MACAT
GREAT WORKS FOR CRITICAL THINKING

Macat is focused on making the ideas of the world's great thinkers accessible and comprehensible to everybody, everywhere, in ways that promote the development of enhanced critical thinking skills.

It works with leading academics from the world's top universities to produce new analyses that focus on the ideas and the impact of the most influential works ever written across a wide variety of academic disciplines. Each of the works that sit at the heart of its growing library is an enduring example of great thinking. But by setting them in context — and looking at the influences that shaped their authors, as well as the responses they provoked — Macat encourages readers to look at these classics and game-changers with fresh eyes. Readers learn to think, engage and challenge their ideas, rather than simply accepting them.

批判性思维与《领导变革》

首要批判性思维技巧：分析

次要批判性思维技巧：评估

约翰·P.科特所著的《领导变革》是一部商业领域的经典著作，也是高屋建瓴地剖析和评估商业案例的典范。

在批评性思维中，分析技巧的关键在于论点的顺序和特征；结合对论点利弊的评估，运用分析技巧，这为公司发展战略和方向研究提供了完美的基础。科特将这些技巧应用于自己对大型和小型企业进行变革指导以提升其绩效的经历。科特的结论本质上很简单：企业转型失败通常缘于糟糕的管理决策。

科特认为，领导层仅有管理技巧是远远不够的。无论哪个行业的公司和组织，在运营中都必须具备坚强的领导力和通用的清晰方案。在重估自身成败经历时，科特运用了分析技巧研究成败经历的顺序和特征，进而评价促发成败的优势和劣势因素。他从中提取了经验教训，从而找到管理者在力图实施变革时常犯的错误。

通过分析和评估过程，科特构建了组织成功变革的八步骤模式——这一模式在 20 年后依然被广泛应用。

CRITICAL THINKING AND *LEADING CHANGE*

- Primary critical thinking skill: ANALYSIS
- Secondary critical thinking skill: EVALUATION

John P. Kotter's *Leading Change* is a classic of business literature, and a strong example of high-level analysis and evaluation.

In critical thinking, analysis is all about the sequence and features of arguments; when combined with evaluation of the strengths and weaknesses of an argument, it provides the perfect basis for understanding corporate strategies and direction. Kotter applied these skills to his own experience of coaching large and small businesses through changes aimed at improving their performance. At heart, his conclusion was simple: unsuccessful transformations usually result from poor management decisions.

Kotter's view was that it was not enough for executives to have management skills. Strong leadership is required, together with a clear process that can be used by all kinds of companies and organizations, no matter what sector they are operating in. Reassessing his own successes and failures alike, Kotter then deployed his analytical skills to understand the sequence and features of both sets of experiences before evaluating the strengths and weaknesses that had contributed to outcomes both good and bad. From there, he distilled lessons that help to identify the common mistakes that managers make when they try to implement change.

The process allowed Kotter to develop an eight-stage model for successful organizational transformation—a model still widely used twenty years on.

《世界思想宝库钥匙丛书》简介

《世界思想宝库钥匙丛书》致力于为一系列在各领域产生重大影响的人文社科类经典著作提供独特的学术探讨。每一本读物都不仅仅是原经典著作的内容摘要，而是介绍并深入研究原经典著作的学术渊源、主要观点和历史影响。这一丛书的目的是提供一套学习资料，以促进读者掌握批判性思维，从而更全面、深刻地去理解重要思想。

每一本读物分为 3 个部分：学术渊源、学术思想和学术影响，每个部分下有 4 个小节。这些章节旨在从各个方面研究原经典著作及其反响。

由于独特的体例，每一本读物不但易于阅读，而且另有一项优点：所有读物的编排体例相同，读者在进行某个知识层面的调查或研究时可交叉参阅多本该丛书中的相关读物，从而开启跨领域研究的路径。

为了方便阅读，每本读物最后还列出了术语表和人名表（在书中则以星号＊标记），此外还有参考文献。

《世界思想宝库钥匙丛书》与剑桥大学合作，理清了批判性思维的要点，即如何通过 6 种技能来进行有效思考。其中 3 种技能让我们能够理解问题，另 3 种技能让我们有能力解决问题。这 6 种技能合称为"批判性思维 PACIER 模式"，它们是：

分析：了解如何建立一个观点；
评估：研究一个观点的优点和缺点；
阐释：对意义所产生的问题加以理解；
创造性思维：提出新的见解，发现新的联系；
解决问题：提出切实有效的解决办法；
理性化思维：创建有说服力的观点。

THE MACAT LIBRARY

The Macat Library is a series of unique academic explorations of seminal works in the humanities and social sciences — books and papers that have had a significant and widely recognised impact on their disciplines. It has been created to serve as much more than just a summary of what lies between the covers of a great book. It illuminates and explores the influences on, ideas of, and impact of that book. Our goal is to offer a learning resource that encourages critical thinking and fosters a better, deeper understanding of important ideas.

Each publication is divided into three Sections: Influences, Ideas, and Impact. Each Section has four Modules. These explore every important facet of the work, and the responses to it.

This Section-Module structure makes a Macat Library book easy to use, but it has another important feature. Because each Macat book is written to the same format, it is possible (and encouraged!) to cross-reference multiple Macat books along the same lines of inquiry or research. This allows the reader to open up interesting interdisciplinary pathways.

To further aid your reading, lists of glossary terms and people mentioned are included at the end of this book (these are indicated by an asterisk [*] throughout) — as well as a list of works cited.

Macat has worked with the University of Cambridge to identify the elements of critical thinking and understand the ways in which six different skills combine to enable effective thinking.

Three allow us to fully understand a problem; three more give us the tools to solve it. Together, these six skills make up the PACIER model of critical thinking. They are:

ANALYSIS — understanding how an argument is built
EVALUATION — exploring the strengths and weaknesses of an argument
INTERPRETATION — understanding issues of meaning
CREATIVE THINKING — coming up with new ideas and fresh connections
PROBLEM-SOLVING — producing strong solutions
REASONING — creating strong arguments

"《世界思想宝库钥匙丛书》提供了独一无二的跨学科学习和研究工具。它介绍那些革新了各自学科研究的经典著作，还邀请全世界一流专家和教育机构进行严谨的分析，为每位读者打开世界顶级教育的大门。"

—— 安德烈亚斯·施莱歇尔，
经济合作与发展组织教育与技能司司长

"《世界思想宝库钥匙丛书》直面大学教育的巨大挑战……他们组建了一支精干而活跃的学者队伍，来推出在研究广度上颇具新意的教学材料。"

—— 布罗尔斯教授、勋爵，剑桥大学前校长

"《世界思想宝库钥匙丛书》的愿景令人赞叹。它通过分析和阐释那些曾深刻影响人类思想以及社会、经济发展的经典文本，提供了新的学习方法。它推动批判性思维，这对于任何社会和经济体来说都是至关重要的。这就是未来的学习方法。"

—— 查尔斯·克拉克阁下，英国前教育大臣

"对于那些影响了各自领域的著作，《世界思想宝库钥匙丛书》能让人们立即了解到围绕那些著作展开的评论性言论，这让该系列图书成为在这些领域从事研究的师生们不可或缺的资源。"

—— 威廉·特朗佐教授，加利福尼亚大学圣地亚哥分校

"Macat offers an amazing first-of-its-kind tool for interdisciplinary learning and research. Its focus on works that transformed their disciplines and its rigorous approach, drawing on the world's leading experts and educational institutions, opens up a world-class education to anyone."

—— Andreas Schleicher, Director for Education and Skills, Organisation for Economic Co-operation and Development

"Macat is taking on some of the major challenges in university education... They have drawn together a strong team of active academics who are producing teaching materials that are novel in the breadth of their approach."

—— Prof Lord Broers, former Vice-Chancellor of the University of Cambridge

"The Macat vision is exceptionally exciting. It focuses upon new modes of learning which analyse and explain seminal texts which have profoundly influenced world thinking and so social and economic development. It promotes the kind of critical thinking which is essential for any society and economy. This is the learning of the future."

—— Rt Hon Charles Clarke, former UK Secretary of State for Education

"The Macat analyses provide immediate access to the critical conversation surrounding the books that have shaped their respective discipline, which will make them an invaluable resource to all of those, students and teachers, working in the field."

—— Prof William Tronzo, University of California at San Diego

TITLE	中文书名	类别
An Analysis of Arjun Appadurai's *Modernity at Large: Cultural Dimensions of Globalization*	解析阿尔君·阿帕杜莱《消失的现代性：全球化的文化维度》	人类学
An Analysis of Claude Lévi-Strauss's *Structural Anthropology*	解析克劳德·列维-斯特劳斯《结构人类学》	人类学
An Analysis of Marcel Mauss's *The Gift*	解析马塞尔·莫斯《礼物》	人类学
An Analysis of Jared M. Diamond's *Guns, Germs, and Steel: The Fate of Human Societies*	解析贾雷德·M.戴蒙德《枪炮、病菌与钢铁：人类社会的命运》	人类学
An Analysis of Clifford Geertz's *The Interpretation of Cultures*	解析克利福德·格尔茨《文化的解释》	人类学
An Analysis of Philippe Ariès's *Centuries of Childhood: A Social History of Family Life*	解析菲力浦·阿利埃斯《儿童的世纪：旧制度下的儿童和家庭生活》	人类学
An Analysis of W. Chan Kim & Renée Mauborgne's *Blue Ocean Strategy*	解析金伟灿/勒妮·莫博涅《蓝海战略》	商业
An Analysis of John P. Kotter's *Leading Change*	解析约翰·P.科特《领导变革》	商业
An Analysis of Michael E. Porter's *Competitive Strategy: Techniques for Analyzing Industries and Competitors*	解析迈克尔·E.波特《竞争战略：分析产业和竞争对手的技术》	商业
An Analysis of Jean Lave & Etienne Wenger's *Situated Learning: Legitimate Peripheral Participation*	解析琼·莱夫/艾蒂纳·温格《情境学习：合法的边缘性参与》	商业
An Analysis of Douglas McGregor's *The Human Side of Enterprise*	解析道格拉斯·麦格雷戈《企业的人性面》	商业
An Analysis of Milton Friedman's *Capitalism and Freedom*	解析米尔顿·弗里德曼《资本主义与自由》	商业
An Analysis of Ludwig von Mises's *The Theory of Money and Credit*	解析路德维希·冯·米塞斯《货币和信用理论》	经济学
An Analysis of Adam Smith's *The Wealth of Nations*	解析亚当·斯密《国富论》	经济学
An Analysis of Thomas Piketty's *Capital in the Twenty-First Century*	解析托马斯·皮凯蒂《21世纪资本论》	经济学
An Analysis of Nassim Nicholas Taleb's *The Black Swan: The Impact of the Highly Improbable*	解析纳西姆·尼古拉斯·塔勒布《黑天鹅：如何应对不可预知的未来》	经济学
An Analysis of Ha-Joon Chang's *Kicking Away the Ladder*	解析张夏准《富国陷阱：发达国家为何踢开梯子》	经济学
An Analysis of Thomas Robert Malthus's *An Essay on the Principle of Population*	解析托马斯·罗伯特·马尔萨斯《人口论》	经济学

An Analysis of John Maynard Keynes's *The General Theory of Employment, Interest and Money*	解析约翰·梅纳德·凯恩斯《就业、利息和货币通论》	经济学
An Analysis of Milton Friedman's *The Role of Monetary Policy*	解析米尔顿·弗里德曼《货币政策的作用》	经济学
An Analysis of Burton G. Malkiel's *A Random Walk Down Wall Street*	解析伯顿·G.马尔基尔《漫步华尔街》	经济学
An Analysis of Friedrich A. Hayek's *The Road to Serfdom*	解析弗里德里希·A.哈耶克《通往奴役之路》	经济学
An Analysis of Charles P. Kindleberger's *Manias, Panics, and Crashes: A History of Financial Crises*	解析查尔斯·P.金德尔伯格《疯狂、惊恐和崩溃：金融危机史》	经济学
An Analysis of Amartya Sen's *Development as Freedom*	解析阿马蒂亚·森《以自由看待发展》	经济学
An Analysis of Rachel Carson's *Silent Spring*	解析蕾切尔·卡森《寂静的春天》	地理学
An Analysis of Charles Darwin's *On the Origin of Species: by Means of Natural Selection, or The Preservation of Favoured Races in the Struggle for Life*	解析查尔斯·达尔文《物种起源》	地理学
An Analysis of World Commission on Environment and Development's *The Brundtland Report: Our Common Future*	解析世界环境与发展委员会《布伦特兰报告：我们共同的未来》	地理学
An Analysis of James E. Lovelock's *Gaia: A New Look at Life on Earth*	解析詹姆斯·E.拉伍洛克《盖娅：地球生命的新视野》	地理学
An Analysis of Paul Kennedy's *The Rise and Fall of the Great Powers: Economic Change and Military Conflict from 1500–2000*	解析保罗·肯尼迪《大国的兴衰：1500—2000年的经济变革与军事冲突》	历史
An Analysis of Janet L. Abu-Lughod's *Before European Hegemony: The World System A. D. 1250–1350*	解析珍妮特·L.阿布-卢格霍德《欧洲霸权之前：1250—1350年的世界体系》	历史
An Analysis of Alfred W. Crosby's *The Columbian Exchange: Biological and Cultural Consequences of 1492*	解析艾尔弗雷德·W.克罗斯比《哥伦布大交换：1492年以后的生物影响和文化冲击》	历史
An Analysis of Tony Judt's *Postwar: A History of Europe since 1945*	解析托尼·朱特《战后欧洲史》	历史
An Analysis of Richard J. Evans's *In Defence of History*	解析理查德·J.艾文斯《捍卫历史》	历史
An Analysis of Eric Hobsbawm's *The Age of Revolution: Europe 1789–1848*	解析艾瑞克·霍布斯鲍姆《革命的年代：欧洲1789—1848年》	历史

An Analysis of Roland Barthes's *Mythologies*	解析罗兰·巴特《神话学》	文学与批判理论
An Analysis of Simone de Beauvoir's *The Second Sex*	解析西蒙娜·德·波伏娃《第二性》	文学与批判理论
An Analysis of Edward W. Said's *Orientalism*	解析爱德华·W. 萨义德《东方主义》	文学与批判理论
An Analysis of Virginia Woolf's *A Room of One's Own*	解析弗吉尼亚·伍尔芙《一间自己的房间》	文学与批判理论
An Analysis of Judith Butler's *Gender Trouble*	解析朱迪斯·巴特勒《性别麻烦》	文学与批判理论
An Analysis of Ferdinand de Saussure's *Course in General Linguistics*	解析费尔迪南·德·索绪尔《普通语言学教程》	文学与批判理论
An Analysis of Susan Sontag's *On Photography*	解析苏珊·桑塔格《论摄影》	文学与批判理论
An Analysis of Walter Benjamin's *The Work of Art in the Age of Mechanical Reproduction*	解析瓦尔特·本雅明《机械复制时代的艺术作品》	文学与批判理论
An Analysis of W. E. B. Du Bois's *The Souls of Black Folk*	解析 W.E.B. 杜波依斯《黑人的灵魂》	文学与批判理论
An Analysis of Plato's *The Republic*	解析柏拉图《理想国》	哲学
An Analysis of Plato's *Symposium*	解析柏拉图《会饮篇》	哲学
An Analysis of Aristotle's *Metaphysics*	解析亚里士多德《形而上学》	哲学
An Analysis of Aristotle's *Nicomachean Ethics*	解析亚里士多德《尼各马可伦理学》	哲学
An Analysis of Immanuel Kant's *Critique of Pure Reason*	解析伊曼努尔·康德《纯粹理性批判》	哲学
An Analysis of Ludwig Wittgenstein's *Philosophical Investigations*	解析路德维希·维特根斯坦《哲学研究》	哲学
An Analysis of G. W. F. Hegel's *Phenomenology of Spirit*	解析 G. W. F. 黑格尔《精神现象学》	哲学
An Analysis of Baruch Spinoza's *Ethics*	解析巴鲁赫·斯宾诺莎《伦理学》	哲学
An Analysis of Hannah Arendt's *The Human Condition*	解析汉娜·阿伦特《人的境况》	哲学
An Analysis of G. E. M. Anscombe's *Modern Moral Philosophy*	解析 G. E. M. 安斯康姆《现代道德哲学》	哲学
An Analysis of David Hume's *An Enquiry Concerning Human Understanding*	解析大卫·休谟《人类理解研究》	哲学

An Analysis of Søren Kierkegaard's *Fear and Trembling*	解析索伦·克尔凯郭尔《恐惧与战栗》	哲学
An Analysis of René Descartes's *Meditations on First Philosophy*	解析勒内·笛卡尔《第一哲学沉思录》	哲学
An Analysis of Friedrich Nietzsche's *On the Genealogy of Morality*	解析弗里德里希·尼采《论道德的谱系》	哲学
An Analysis of Gilbert Ryle's *The Concept of Mind*	解析吉尔伯特·赖尔《心的概念》	哲学
An Analysis of Thomas Kuhn's *The Structure of Scientific Revolutions*	解析托马斯·库恩《科学革命的结构》	哲学
An Analysis of John Stuart Mill's *Utilitarianism*	解析约翰·斯图亚特·穆勒《功利主义》	哲学
An Analysis of Aristotle's *Politics*	解析亚里士多德《政治学》	政治学
An Analysis of Niccolò Machiavelli's *The Prince*	解析尼科洛·马基雅维利《君主论》	政治学
An Analysis of Karl Marx's *Capital*	解析卡尔·马克思《资本论》	政治学
An Analysis of Benedict Anderson's *Imagined Communities*	解析本尼迪克特·安德森《想象的共同体》	政治学
An Analysis of Samuel P. Huntington's *The Clash of Civilizations and the Remaking of World Order*	解析塞缪尔·P.亨廷顿《文明的冲突与世界秩序的重建》	政治学
An Analysis of Alexis de Tocqueville's *Democracy in America*	解析阿列克西·德·托克维尔《论美国的民主》	政治学
An Analysis of John A. Hobson's *Imperialism: A Study*	解析约翰·A.霍布森《帝国主义》	政治学
An Analysis of Thomas Paine's *Common Sense*	解析托马斯·潘恩《常识》	政治学
An Analysis of John Rawls's *A Theory of Justice*	解析约翰·罗尔斯《正义论》	政治学
An Analysis of Francis Fukuyama's *The End of History and the Last Man*	解析弗朗西斯·福山《历史的终结与最后的人》	政治学
An Analysis of John Locke's *Two Treatises of Government*	解析约翰·洛克《政府论》	政治学
An Analysis of Sun Tzu's *The Art of War*	解析孙武《孙子兵法》	政治学
An Analysis of Henry Kissinger's *World Order: Reflections on the Character of Nations and the Course of History*	解析亨利·基辛格《世界秩序》	政治学
An Analysis of Jean-Jacques Rousseau's *The Social Contract*	解析让-雅克·卢梭《社会契约论》	政治学

An Analysis of Odd Arne Westad's *The Global Cold War: Third World Interventions and the Making of Our Times*	解析文安立《全球冷战：美苏对第三世界的干涉与当代世界的形成》	政治学
An Analysis of Sigmund Freud's *The Interpretation of Dreams*	解析西格蒙德·弗洛伊德《梦的解析》	心理学
An Analysis of William James' *The Principles of Psychology*	解析威廉·詹姆斯《心理学原理》	心理学
An Analysis of Philip Zimbardo's *The Lucifer Effect*	解析菲利普·津巴多《路西法效应》	心理学
An Analysis of Leon Festinger's *A Theory of Cognitive Dissonance*	解析利昂·费斯汀格《认知失调论》	心理学
An Analysis of Richard H. Thaler & Cass R. Sunstein's *Nudge: Improving Decisions about Health, Wealth, and Happiness*	解析理查德·H. 泰勒 / 卡斯·R. 桑斯坦《助推：如何做出有关健康、财富和幸福的更优决策》	心理学
An Analysis of Gordon Allport's *The Nature of Prejudice*	解析高尔登·奥尔波特《偏见的本质》	心理学
An Analysis of Steven Pinker's *The Better Angels of Our Nature: Why Violence Has Declined*	解析斯蒂芬·平克《人性中的善良天使：暴力为什么会减少》	心理学
An Analysis of Stanley Milgram's *Obedience to Authority*	解析斯坦利·米尔格拉姆《对权威的服从》	心理学
An Analysis of Betty Friedan's *The Feminine Mystique*	解析贝蒂·弗里丹《女性的奥秘》	心理学
An Analysis of David Riesman's *The Lonely Crowd: A Study of the Changing American Character*	解析大卫·理斯曼《孤独的人群：美国人社会性格演变之研究》	社会学
An Analysis of Franz Boas's *Race, Language and Culture*	解析弗朗兹·博厄斯《种族、语言与文化》	社会学
An Analysis of Pierre Bourdieu's *Outline of a Theory of Practice*	解析皮埃尔·布尔迪厄《实践理论大纲》	社会学
An Analysis of Max Weber's *The Protestant Ethic and the Spirit of Capitalism*	解析马克斯·韦伯《新教伦理与资本主义精神》	社会学
An Analysis of Jane Jacobs's *The Death and Life of Great American Cities*	解析简·雅各布斯《美国大城市的死与生》	社会学
An Analysis of C. Wright Mills's *The Sociological Imagination*	解析C. 赖特·米尔斯《社会学的想象力》	社会学
An Analysis of Robert E. Lucas Jr.'s *Why Doesn't Capital Flow from Rich to Poor Countries?*	解析小罗伯特·E. 卢卡斯《为何资本不从富国流向穷国？》	社会学

An Analysis of Émile Durkheim's *On Suicide*	解析埃米尔·迪尔凯姆《自杀论》	社会学
An Analysis of Eric Hoffer's *The True Believer: Thoughts on the Nature of Mass Movements*	解析埃里克·霍弗《狂热分子：群众运动圣经》	社会学
An Analysis of Jared M. Diamond's *Collapse: How Societies Choose to Fail or Survive*	解析贾雷德·M.戴蒙德《大崩溃：社会如何选择兴亡》	社会学
An Analysis of Michel Foucault's *The History of Sexuality Vol. 1: The Will to Knowledge*	解析米歇尔·福柯《性史（第一卷）：求知意志》	社会学
An Analysis of Michel Foucault's *Discipline and Punish*	解析米歇尔·福柯《规训与惩罚》	社会学
An Analysis of Richard Dawkins's *The Selfish Gene*	解析理查德·道金斯《自私的基因》	社会学
An Analysis of Antonio Gramsci's *Prison Notebooks*	解析安东尼奥·葛兰西《狱中札记》	社会学
An Analysis of Augustine's *Confessions*	解析奥古斯丁《忏悔录》	神学
An Analysis of C. S. Lewis's *The Abolition of Man*	解析 C. S. 路易斯《人之废》	神学

图书在版编目（CIP）数据

解析约翰·P.科特《领导变革》: 汉、英 / 雅米娜·萨尔曼（Yaamina Salman），尼克·布罗顿（Nick Broten）著；曾文雄译.—上海：上海外语教育出版社，2020
（世界思想宝库钥匙丛书）
ISBN 978-7-5446-6389-2

Ⅰ.①解… Ⅱ.①雅… ②尼… ③曾… Ⅲ.①领导学－研究－汉、英 Ⅳ.①C933

中国版本图书馆CIP数据核字（2020）第056447号

This Chinese-English bilingual edition of *An Analysis of John P. Kotter's* Leading Change is published by arrangement with Macat International Limited.
Licensed for sale throughout the world.

本书汉英双语版由Macat国际有限公司授权上海外语教育出版社有限公司出版。供在全世界范围内发行、销售。

图字：09 - 2018 - 549

出版发行：**上海外语教育出版社**
（上海外国语大学内）　邮编：200083
电　　　话：021-65425300（总机）
电子邮箱：bookinfo@sflep.com.cn
网　　　址：http://www.sflep.com
责任编辑：张　婕

印　　　刷：启东市人民印刷有限公司
开　　　本：890×1240　1/32　印张 5.375　字数 111千字
版　　　次：2020 年 8月第 1版　2020 年 8月第 1次印刷
印　　　数：2 100 册

书　　　号：ISBN 978-7-5446-6389-2
定　　　价：30.00 元
本版图书如有印装质量问题，可向本社调换
质量服务热线：4008-213-263　电子邮箱：editorial@sflep.com